COMPARISON OF THE INVASION OF CRETE AND
THE PROPOSED INVASION OF MALTA

A thesis presented to the Faculty of the U.S. Army
Command and General Staff College in partial
fulfillment of the requirements for the
degree

MASTER OF MILITARY ART AND SCIENCE
Military History

by

STEPHEN L. W. KAVANAUGH, MAJ, USA
B.A., Virginia Military Institute, Lexington, VA, 1994

Fort Leavenworth, Kansas
2006

Approved for public release; distribution is unlimited.

Report Documentation Page			Form Approved OMB No. 0704-0188

Public reporting burden for the collection of information is estimated to average 1 hour per response, including the time for reviewing instructions, searching existing data sources, gathering and maintaining the data needed, and completing and reviewing the collection of information. Send comments regarding this burden estimate or any other aspect of this collection of information, including suggestions for reducing this burden, to Washington Headquarters Services, Directorate for Information Operations and Reports, 1215 Jefferson Davis Highway, Suite 1204, Arlington VA 22202-4302. Respondents should be aware that notwithstanding any other provision of law, no person shall be subject to a penalty for failing to comply with a collection of information if it does not display a currently valid OMB control number.

1. REPORT DATE **16 JUN 2006**	2. REPORT TYPE	3. DATES COVERED
4. TITLE AND SUBTITLE **Comparison of the invasion of Crete and the proposed invasion in Malta.**		5a. CONTRACT NUMBER
		5b. GRANT NUMBER
		5c. PROGRAM ELEMENT NUMBER
6. AUTHOR(S) **Stephen L.W. Kavanaugh**		5d. PROJECT NUMBER
		5e. TASK NUMBER
		5f. WORK UNIT NUMBER
7. PERFORMING ORGANIZATION NAME(S) AND ADDRESS(ES) **US Army Command and General Staff College,1 Reynolds Ave.,Fort Leavenworth,KS,66027-1352**		8. PERFORMING ORGANIZATION REPORT NUMBER **ATZL-SWD-GD**
9. SPONSORING/MONITORING AGENCY NAME(S) AND ADDRESS(ES)		10. SPONSOR/MONITOR'S ACRONYM(S)
		11. SPONSOR/MONITOR'S REPORT NUMBER(S)

12. DISTRIBUTION/AVAILABILITY STATEMENT
Approved for public release; distribution unlimited.

13. SUPPLEMENTARY NOTES

14. ABSTRACT
In 1941, after the conquest of Yugoslavia and Greece, senior German military leaders were considering two airborne operations, one for the invasion of Crete and the other for the invasion of Malta. The invasion of Crete was executed from 20 May to 1 June 1941 with heavy German losses. The invasion of Malta never took place even though the senior military leaders in the Oberkommando der Wehrmacht (OKW) recommended invading Malta over Crete because of its strategic importance, but were overridden by Adolf Hitler. A year later, while the North Africa campaign was being conducted, another invasion was planned for Malta, but within a few weeks of executing the plan it too was postponed and eventually cancelled. The primary focus of this research is to establish why in 1941 Crete was invaded, but Malta was not. The secondary focus is to establish why one year later a second planned invasion of Malta was rejected and abandoned, and what were the strategic repercussions of not invading Malta. The Axis never captured Malta, and the offensive capability of Malta was never destroyed, thus leading to the defeat of all Axis forces in North Africa.

15. SUBJECT TERMS

16. SECURITY CLASSIFICATION OF:			17. LIMITATION OF ABSTRACT **1**	18. NUMBER OF PAGES **126**	19a. NAME OF RESPONSIBLE PERSON
a. REPORT **unclassified**	b. ABSTRACT **unclassified**	c. THIS PAGE **unclassified**			

Standard Form 298 (Rev. 8-98)
Prescribed by ANSI Std Z39-18

MASTER OF MILITARY ART AND SCIENCE

THESIS APPROVAL PAGE

Name of Candidate: MAJ Stephen L. W. Kavanaugh

Thesis Title: Comparison of the Invasion of Crete and the Proposed Invasion of Malta

Approved by:

_____, Thesis Committee Chair
Jonathan M. House, Ph.D.

_____, Member
Mr. Bob A. King, M.B.A., M.A.

_____, Member
Mr. Herbert F. Merrick, M.S.

Accepted this 16th day of June 2006 by:

_____, Director, Graduate Degree Programs
Robert F. Baumann, Ph.D.

The opinions and conclusions expressed herein are those of the student author and do not necessarily represent the views of the U.S. Army Command and General Staff College or any other governmental agency. (References to this study should include the foregoing statement.)

ABSTRACT

COMPARISON OF THE INVASION OF CRETE AND THE PROPOSED INVASION OF MALTA by MAJ Stephen L. W. Kavanaugh, 115 pages.

In 1941, after the conquest of Yugoslavia and Greece, senior German military leaders were considering two airborne operations, one for the invasion of Crete and the other for the invasion of Malta. The invasion of Crete was executed from 20 May to 1 June 1941 with heavy German losses. The invasion of Malta never took place even though the senior military leaders in the Oberkommando der Wehrmacht (OKW) recommended invading Malta over Crete because of its strategic importance, but were overridden by Adolf Hitler. A year later, while the North Africa campaign was being conducted, another invasion was planned for Malta, but within a few weeks of executing the plan it too was postponed and eventually cancelled. The primary focus of this research is to establish why in 1941 Crete was invaded, but Malta was not. The secondary focus is to establish why one year later a second planned invasion of Malta was rejected and abandoned, and what were the strategic repercussions of not invading Malta. The Axis never captured Malta, and the offensive capability of Malta was never destroyed, thus leading to the defeat of all Axis forces in North Africa.

ACKNOWLEDGEMENTS

I would like to thank the ever-present support and patience of my family, especially my wife Michelle, because without her understanding this project would never have succeeded. COL Rainer Waelde and Dr. Wayne Lutton, whose assistance with research is greatly appreciated. I want to thank my committee Dr. Jonathan House, Mr. Bob King, and Mr. Herb Merrick for their support and assistance. Even through their busy schedules they provided guidance and suggestions that enabled this project to reach its successful conclusion. Finally, Mrs. Helen Davis who reviews every MMAS thesis and still managed to treat this thesis as if it was the most important to her.

DEDICATION

To my wife, Michelle; and my sons, Conner and Aidan, for their sacrifice on weekends and evenings while I completed this project and missed part of the best year of my life.

TABLE OF CONTENTS

Page

MASTER OF MILITARY ART AND SCIENCE THESIS APPROVAL PAGE ii

ABSTRACT iii

ACKNOWLEDGEMENTS iv

DEDICATION v

ACRONYMS AND DEFINITIONS viii

ILLUSTRATIONS x

PREFACE xi

CHAPTER 1 MALTA 1

    Introduction 1
    Location 2
    Topography 3
    History 4
    Security 6

CHAPTER 2 STRATEGIC SETTING 9

    Great Britain 10
    Germany 13
    Italy 18

CHAPTER 3 OPERATION MERCURY (INVASION OF CRETE) 32

    Location and Topography 32
    Operational Situation 33
    Planning 37
    Intelligence 40
    Logistics 41
    Operational 42
    Results and Lessons Learned 46
        Results 46
        Lessons Learned 48
    Conclusion 50

CHAPTER 4 ATTACKING AND DEFENDING MALTA 54

    1940 54
    1941 63
    Resupplying Malta 70
    Strategic Update 72
    1942 75

CHAPTER 5 OPERATION HERCULES 85

    Planning of Operation 85
    Hercules: The Plan 89
    Hercules: Training 92
    Hercules: Invasion and Logistical Support 95
    Rommel Seizes Tobruk 96
    Hercules: Cancelled 98
    What Happened to Malta? 102

CHAPTER 6 CONCLUSION 106

    Why Not Malta? 106

BIBLIOGRAPHY 111

INITIAL DISTRIBUTION LIST 113

CERTIFICATION FOR MMAS DISTRIBUTION STATEMENT 114

ACRONYMS AND DEFINITIONS

Commando Supremo	Italian Military High Command
DAK	Deutsches Afrika Korps, German Africa Corps
DIME	Elements of National Power (Diplomatic, Information, Military, Economic)
Flieger	Flying, usually translated as Airborne
Fliegerkorps	Air Corps
FJR	Fallschirmjäger Regiment, Parachute Infantry Regiment
Gebirgs	Mountain
General der Flieger	Lieutenant General (Luftwaffe)
GeneralFeldmarschall	General of the Army
Generalleuntant	Lieutenant General
Generalmajor	Major General
Großadmiral	Fleet Admiral
Luftflotte	Air Fleet, Air Force: ex. 4th Air Force
Luftlande	Airlanding
Luftlande Sturmregiment	Airlanding assault regiment
OB South	Oberbefehlshaber South, Commander-in-Chief South
OKH	Ober Kommando der Heeres, German Army High Command
OKL	Ober Kommando die Luftwaffe, German Air Force High Command
OKM	Ober Kommando der Kriegsmarine, German Navy High Command
OKW	Ober Kommando der Wehrmacht, German Armed Forces High Command

RDF	Radio Direction Finder
Regia Aeuronautica	Royal (Italian) Air Force
Regia Esercito	Royal (Italian) Army
Regia Marina	Royal (Italian) Navy

ILLUSTRATIONS

Page

Figure 1. Unit Symbols xi

Figure 2. Map of Europe and Mediterranean Theater 3

Figure 3. Axis convoy routes 1941-1942 67

Figure 4. Diagram of Hercules Plan 90

Figure 5. Axis Order of Battle for Operation Hercules 94

PREFACE

Note: In order to maintain consistency throughout this thesis "Europe" refers to the European mainland from France to the Soviet Union, to include the Balkans and the Mediterranean Sea. North Africa refers to the area of Africa that is along the Mediterranean Sea from Tunisia to Egypt. This is to be used primarily at the strategic level. The "Mediterranean Theater" refers to the Mediterranean Sea, the Balkans, and North Africa at primarily the operational level of warfare.

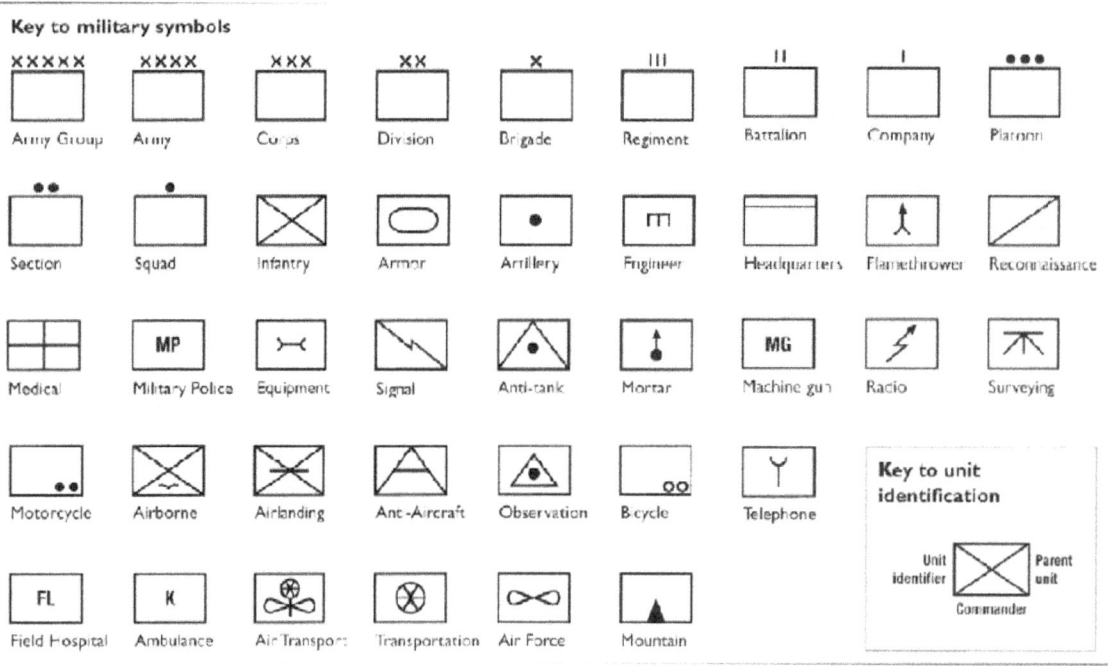

Figure 1. Unit Symbols
Source: Bruce Quarrie, *German Airborne Divisions: Mediterranean Theatre, 1942-1945* (Oxford, England: Osprey Publishing, 2005), 2.

CHAPTER 1

MALTA

Introduction

In the Pacific Theater of Operations during World War II there were many islands that were considered by both the United States and Japan to be vital and thus warranted vast expenditures of resources to attack and defend. Some of these islands were Guadalcanal, Tarawa, Guam, Tinian, and Iwo Jima. All of these islands had an importance at the strategic and operational level of warfare in World War II. These islands were in a position that could directly affect the offensive capability of one side, interdict the sea and air lines of communication within the theater, or serve as an airbase from which to conduct either or both fighter and bombing operations.

In the European Theater of Operations, due primarily to the terrain, only a few islands had important roles in the conduct of operations. However, there was one island in the Mediterranean Sea that was to have strong strategic and operational implications on the European mainland, in the Mediterranean Sea, and in North Africa. This island was Malta. Because of its location Malta was to influence the way that Great Britain, Italy, and Germany conducted operations throughout Europe until 1943.

Throughout the war in the Mediterranean Theatre of Operations Malta was a huge stumbling block for Italy and Germany. Many attempts were made by Italy and Germany through their respective air forces to render the base ineffective as a platform to conduct air and naval operations. The problem was that whenever the air offensives were reduced or paused the British found a way to make Malta operational and continue to attack Italian and German convoys supporting operations in North Africa. However, the Axis never executed an operation to seize Malta and therefore take it away from the British and make it an operational base for the Axis forces to conduct offensive operations. This information forces the following question: Why did the Axis expend so much manpower and materiel to neutralize the island, but not to seize it and totally prevent its use? What was the strategic or operational reasoning why Italy and Germany never invaded the island? This study attempts to answer this question, and also try to see if their reasoning was correct.

Location

The island of Malta is located almost directly in the middle of the Mediterranean Sea. The Malta archipelago consists of three islands (Malta, Gozo, Comino) and is located just 56 miles south of Sicily and 225 miles from the coast of Tunisia. The highest elevation on the main island is 846 feet. The width of the main island, Malta, varies between 6 and 7 1/2 miles. Of Malta's twenty-eight miles of coastline, nineteen, according to the British, were suitable for the landing of troops.[1] Of the other two key British bases in the Mediterranean, Gibraltar is about 1,000 miles away and Alexandria some 820 miles.(see figure 2) Malta has a total area of 121.9 square miles (315.6 square kilometers), and the main island of Malta is 94.8 square miles in area.[2] With a population of some 300,000, Malta had a population density of over 2,300 per square mile, rising to 49,504 per square mile in the urban districts.[3] This population density made it one of the most densely populated places in the world in World War II.[4]

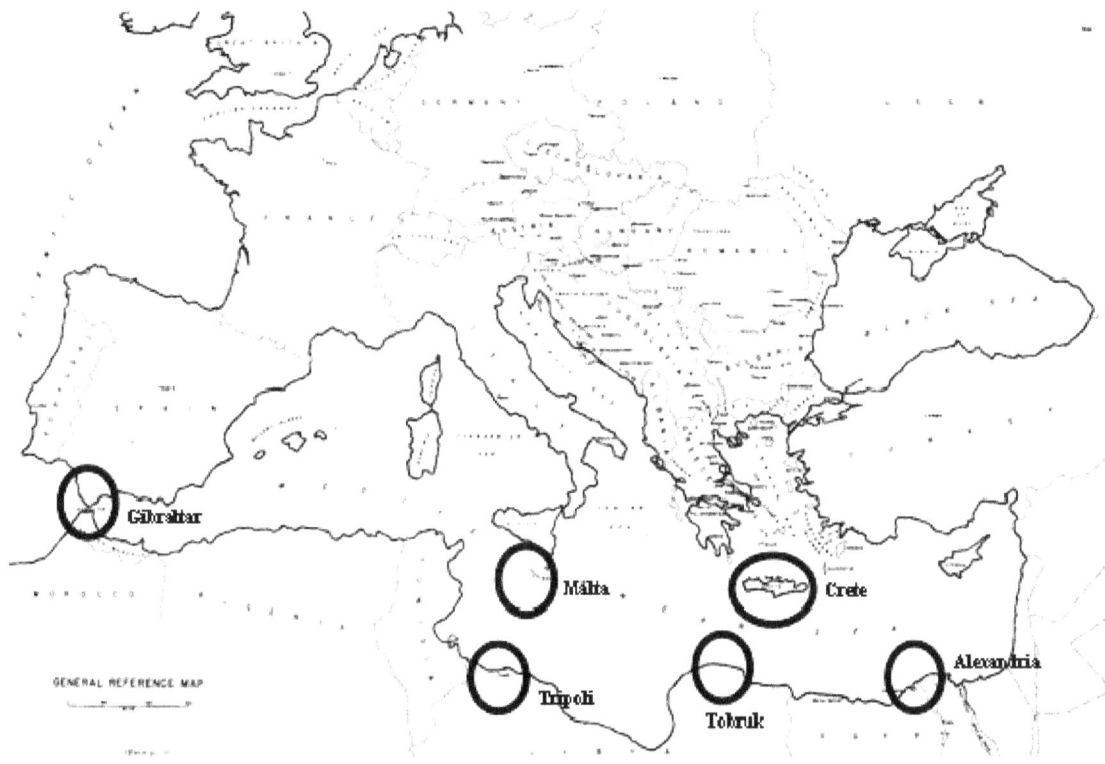

Figure 2. Map of Europe and Mediterranean Theater
Source: Department of the Army, Department of the Army Pamphlet 20-260, *The German Campaigns in the Balkans (Spring 1941)* (Historical study, Department of the Army, November 1953), 1.

Topography

At first glance the main island seems to comprise just a featureless rock plateau, but in fact there are a number of topographical regions. In the west is a high limestone plateau, falling away in steps on all sides and providing only for some sparse grazing for sheep and goats. To the north, an escarpment edges the plateau, while in the east it is cut by a number of small valleys. Within these lower-lying areas the soil is good for crops and by making full use of irrigation they are intensively cultivated. North of the plateau there are ridges and depressions, which are continued in the islands of Comino and Gozo. In the south and southeast of Malta there are gently undulating uplands, which is where many of the people live. The coastline has high cliffs in the southwest, gentle bays in the northwest and wide beaches in the north.[5]

The Grand Harbor of Valetta is a natural deep-water harbor with a depth of 25 meters, which has ensured its economic and strategic importance over the centuries. One of Malta's major problems is that it is badly supplied with drinking water. There are no rivers or lakes, so it depends very much on its winter rainfall. This has over the years provided underground stores of fresh water. The hot, dry summers and mild, wet winters are influenced by the trade winds that blow in from the French Mediterranean coast, the mistral and, less pleasant, the xlokk that brings sultry, warm and humid air from North Africa, particularly in the late summer/early autumn.[6] This influenced the directions that sailing ships approached the island, and could have determined the direction of approach for transport aircraft carrying paratroopers.

History

Malta's history has been one of occupation by other countries in order to gain an advantage within the Mediterranean for economic and military importance. Ever since earliest recorded times Malta has been looked upon as "the navel of the inland sea", long providing a natural bridge between Europe and Africa. Malta has been inhabited since as early as 4000 B.C. By 218 B.C. it was ruled by the Roman Empire. During the period of Roman control it is said that Saint Paul was shipwrecked on the island in A.D. 59 and converted the population to Christianity. The Romans remained in control of Malta, or "Melita" as they called it, until it was taken over by Arabs in A.D. 870 The Arabs held the island until 1091 when the Norman ruler of Sicily defeated them. With the Arab defeat Roman Catholicism was reestablished. During and after the Middle Ages the island again gained importance within the Mediterranean. The Ottoman Empire attempted to capture the islands from the Knights of St. John, who held Malta for close to 270 years, in the Great Siege of 1565. During this siege the Knights held off the Turkish fleet from May to September of that year. The Knights would continue to hold the islands until surrendering them to Napoleon and the French in 1798. Britain would next blockade Malta and then occupy the island in 1800.[7]

Malta's location in the central Mediterranean Sea made it as important strategically as Gibraltar was to the British. Gibraltar controlled access to the Mediterranean Sea. Malta, however, was able to provide the British with the ability to control access to three seas; the Western Mediterranean, the Adriatic, and the Aegean through the Eastern Mediterranean. Because of Britain's naval strength it was able to influence the strategic actions of the three powers that bordered the Mediterranean; France, Spain, and Italy. As long as Great Britain possessed Malta and Gibraltar it would be the dominant sea power in the Mediterranean.[8]

Malta had been the most important British naval base in the Mediterranean since its capture from the French. It possessed a dry dock and complete repair facilities capable of handling the largest ships in the service of the Royal Navy.[9] It also had ample equipment reserves and resources, sufficient to maintain the British Mediterranean Fleet that was based at Malta and which, between World War I and World War II, was second in strength only to the Home Fleet. The security of the base, symbolized by the presence of up to four battleships and their attendant cruisers and destroyers anchored in Grand Harbor, seemed unshakeable until the mid 1930s.[10]

Security

After the Ethiopian crisis of 1935, it became increasingly clear to Britain that Italy could not be relied upon to remain a friendly power. With Italian airbases in Sicily, the Regia Aeronautica was only twenty minutes flying time away from Malta. And it should be recalled that in the mid-to-late 1930s, Italy had what was considered to be a first-class air force, given the standards of the time. The British War Cabinet concluded that the threat of aerial bombardment jeopardized the security of Malta to such an extent that in July 1937 the cabinet decided to develop Alexandria as the main base of the Mediterranean Fleet.[11] In the middle of 1936 the Italian Consul-General was expelled for organizing espionage and subversion and thereafter Italy appears to have abandoned any further attempts at spying or sabotage.[12] From this point the British took measures to increase the security of the island base.

In July 1939, the British Committee of Imperial Defense authorized an increase of antiaircraft defenses for Malta. The Army and Royal Air Force protested that it was a waste of money and equipment to try to improve the air defenses of a fleet base that was so obviously vulnerable. Following a technical evaluation, the Committee decided to base four fighter squadrons on the island, along with 112 heavy and 60 light antiaircraft guns, supported by 24 searchlights. In April 1939, Malta was one of the first overseas bases to receive a new Radio Direction Finder (RDF)--as radar was then referred to.[13]

Nevertheless, Malta was practically defenseless in June 1940 when the war commenced in the Mediterranean and could have easily been taken by Italy, who had just declared war on Great Britain. Very few of the authorized increases in the defense had been delivered. The searchlights had arrived, but only 34 of the heavy guns and 8 of the light ones. None of the fighter squadrons were on hand. Manning the coastal and antiaircraft batteries were the men of the Royal Malta Artillery and the King's Own Malta Regiment. A few days before Mussolini declared war, Admiral Cunningham sent the old monitor HMS *Terror* to La Valetta, Malta's main harbor, to add its guns to the defense. Thus Italy's failure to capture Malta in a *coup de main* at the outset gave the British an opportunity to reinforce the base. The consequences of this failure on the part of Mussolini became more and more evident as the war progressed.[14]

On Italy's entry into the war Italian residents and some pro-Italian Maltese were interned and there was no sign of any fifth column activity or resumed espionage until May 1942. In that month Carmelo Borg Pisani landed on the southeast coast in an Italian E-boat with a wireless radio set, maps, money, and instructions to report to Italian naval intelligence on British operational movements, morale, and food supplies. Pisani was immediately captured by a patrol from the 1st Dorsets. He was handed over to military intelligence and later executed in November 1942 as a spy. After this the Axis made no further attempts to land spies.[15]

For centuries prior to the Second World War Malta was a strategic island. It is relevant to see what the strategic situation was for each of the significant powers in the Mediterranean Theater of Operations. These powers are defined as the countries of Great Britain, Italy, and Germany. Each had different goals at the strategic level, and therefore each had a different view of Malta and how it would impact their strategic and operational conduct of the war.

[1] Wayne Lutton, *Malta and the Mediterranean: A Study in The Allied and Axis Strategy, Planning, and Intelligence during The Second World War* (Ann Arbor, MI: University Microfilms International. 1983), 27.

[2] George Forty. *Battle for Malta*, (Hersham, England: Ian Allen Publishing. 2003), p. 14.

[3] Lutton, 69.

[4] Forty, 17.

[5] Ibid., 15.

[6] Ibid., 15.

[7] Ibid., 14.

[8] John Keegan, *The Price of Admiralty: The Evolution of Naval Warfare* (London: Penguin Press, 1990), 11-13.

[9] Lutton, 28.

[10] Forty, 14.

[11] Lutton, 28.

[12] Forty, 17.

[13] Lutton, 28-29.

[14] Ibid., 27 & 29.

[15] Forty, 17.

CHAPTER 2

STRATEGIC SETTING

Before looking at the operations that occurred on, from, and against Malta and the proposed invasion of Malta, there are two important factors that need to be addressed. The first was the strategic situation of the three main powers in the Mediterranean Theater--Great Britain, Italy, and Germany--from 1940 through the end of 1941. Malta affected each of these nations and their armed forces. The second factor, described in chapter 3 was Operation Mercury, the invasion of Crete. It is necessary to talk about the planning, outcome, and lessons learned from this invasion at the strategic and operational level in order to get a better understanding of how the Ober Kommando der Wehrmacht (OKW) and Commando Supremo, the Italian Military High Command, planned to execute the invasion of Malta, and why Hitler and Mussolini ultimately decided not to conduct Operation Hercules, the airborne and seaborne invasion of Malta.

The Mediterranean Sea and surrounding land areas were not considered a theater of war until June 1940, when Italy declared war on Great Britain and France. Once Italy declares war a series of events took place that pushed the Mediterranean Theater and specifically Malta into the forefront of military operations by the three countries already listed and ultimately by the United States. This chapter ends with 1941 because to go into further detail would detract from the operations against Malta in 1940 and 1941, and because as the second proposed invasion of Malta, Operation Hercules, is discussed, I will give an update on the strategic situation and how it affected the planning and execution of the invasion at the time.

It would be hard to say who had more at stake in the loss or capture of the tiny island fortress from 1940 through 1943. Great Britain felt it was necessary to hold onto Malta in order to maintain a link between Gibraltar in the west and Alexandria in the east in turn ensuring the survival of its troops in North Africa and the Middle East. The loss of Malta would have forced Britain to move troops and supplies completely around the continent of Africa, a journey of several thousand miles. Italy felt it was necessary to attack Malta by air in order to neutralize the island and permit the movement of supply convoys to Libya and the Italian forces fighting there. Germany at first had no desire to interfere with the plans of Italy and did not want to be bothered with Italy's *"Mare Nostrum"* while planning for the invasion of Great Britain and later the invasion of Russia. Circumstances later forced Hitler to come to the aid of his failing ally in order to keep Italy in the war and Mussolini in power.

Great Britain

Malta was controlled by Great Britain prior to and throughout the war; so let us look at the British situation first. In 1940 Great Britain was one of two countries actively at war with Germany, with France being the other. Since Italy was not yet involved in the war there was very little that the British had to fear about the loss of Malta. With that in mind the two allies had a cooperative alliance for the defense of the Mediterranean in case Italy did enter the war, but like everything else that was done prior to war commencing in Europe it was not given the top priority.

At the beginning of 1940 Great Britain was not involved in active fighting on the mainland of Europe, but was fighting Germany at sea in the Battle of the Atlantic, a campaign that would affect decisions of the Royal Navy throughout the war. In April

1940 Great Britain had to react to the German invasion of Denmark and more importantly to the invasion of Norway because it gave Germany a safe staging area for surface ships into the North Sea and into the Atlantic Ocean, which threatened convoys transiting to Britain. It was this dismal invasion that finally caused Winston Churchill to replace Neville Chamberlain as Great Britain's Prime Minister on 10 May 1940.[1] That same day Great Britain and France found themselves having to deal with the German invasion of France and the Low Countries, Belgium, Holland, and Luxembourg. Unable to stop the German advance through northern France, British and other allied forces were ordered to move to the channel ports to be evacuated. Operation Dynamo, the evacuation of Dunkirk, began on 27 May and concluded on 4 June with the evacuation of approximately 220,000 British and 120,000 French troops[2]. Six days later Italy declared war on Great Britain and France. This action forced Great Britain to shift some strategic focus to the Mediterranean Theater, including the island of Malta, and Egypt, which contained 40,000 British and Dominion troops.

With France defeated and occupied by Germany, Great Britain stood alone in the war against Germany, and immediately began planning for the Battle of Britain that it knew would come at some point. The air defense of Great Britain was the primary focus. The British War Cabinet concluded on 6 June that any fighters sent to the Mediterranean would be better used to defend Alexandria rather than Malta. However, two weeks later, Prime Minister Churchill vetoed a proposal to abandon Malta and the eastern Mediterranean and withdraw Admiral Cunningham's fleet to Gibraltar.[3] Both planes and pilots were in short supply but because of Churchill's insistence on defending Malta, aircraft and crews were made available to be sent to the island. From the outset of the war in the Mediterranean, Malta was regarded as one of Britain's most vital bases. Aside from its military utility, the island was a symbol of British sea power and of the will to resist the Axis dictators. So, if Mussolini gave little thought to Malta and its potential threat to his North African supply lines, such was not the case with Churchill and the British Admiralty.[4]

For the remainder of 1940 Great Britain stood alone in the Mediterranean against Italy and was able to win some strong victories. By the close of 1940 British General Percival Wavell in Egypt had fought a campaign against the Italian forces in North Africa and captured 130,000 Italian prisoners, ultimately taking most of Libya from the Italians to including the port city of Tobruk.[5]

As 1941 began the outlook for Great Britain was still uncertain, but was better then in 1940; however, by the end of the year, the outlook became very bleak again. In February 1941 Britain was facing not only Italian but also strong German forces in North Africa that would result in another long campaign across Libya and parts of Egypt for the entire year. The battle of the Atlantic was still going strong, but the convoy system and Lend-Lease program, which began in March 1941 from the United States, was helping to lower losses and increase the supplies getting through. The spring of 1941 saw Great Britain shifting forces from North Africa to Greece to stop the German invasion of the Balkans. This was followed by two evacuations similar to Dunkirk. The first was the evacuation of 43,000 troops from Greece to Crete and Egypt and the second, following the German airborne invasion of Crete, was the evacuation of 14,800 British, Greek and Allied soldiers from Crete to Egypt. With the defeat in Greece and Crete, British forces were only visible on one part of mainland Europe, Gibraltar. The Gibraltar- Malta- Alexandria line was to serve as a strategic hinge in the defense of Great Britain's assets.

The German bombing campaign against British cities, the Blitz, and the battle of the Atlantic both continued throughout 1941, as did the fighting in North Africa against Rommel's Africa Corps. But so far the war had not involved Great Britain's Pacific oriented territories and therefore had not forced the proper allocations of personnel or the proper supplies to defend its Asian empire. This changed in December 1941 with the Japanese attack on the United States fleet at Pearl Harbor and the British garrisons in Malaya, Hong Kong, Shanghai, and elsewhere.[6] Along with attacks against British possessions came attacks that required the evacuation of Australian forces in North Africa in order to defend Australia against possible Japanese attacks.[7]

At the close of 1941 Great Britain's forces were stretched more then either Italy or Germany since they were involved in combat operations on a true global scale. However, Britain still managed to find a way to defend one of its smallest territories and cause it to be a thorn in the side of the Axis powers in Europe.

Germany

Even after Italy's entry into the war, Germany had little to no interest in the Mediterranean Theater. According to Hitler the Mediterranean was entirely Mussolini's affair. Hitler was satisfied that the Italians had everything under control and would soon be able to "see off" the tiny British forces in the area of Mussolini's lake. However, when he realized the incompetence of the Italians and their inability to cope with Greece and Great Britain he felt forced to shift badly needed resources.[8] This situation between the

Italian and German Armed forces and specifically between Hitler and Mussolini will be discussed at a later point as the planning for operations against Malta began to take shape.

At the beginning of 1940 Germany was in control of most of continental Europe. Germany had conducted a successful campaign against Poland in September 1939. Just prior to that campaign Germany and the Soviet Union had surprised the western allies by signing a non-aggression pact, thereby securing Germany's eastern flank from possible attack at least for the time being. At the beginning of 1940 in the west there was a state of war, but no combat on the continent of Europe. What existed was the *"Sitzkrieg"* or "phony war." Germany's Navy (Kriegsmarine) and more specifically the U-boat force under the command of Admiral Karl Dönitz was very active, conducting unrestricted submarine warfare against Great Britain's merchant fleet and the Royal Navy in an attempt to strangle Great Britain's lifeline to the outside world and force her to surrender.

On 9 April 1940, Germany invaded and captured Denmark and Norway and occupied these countries with approximately 500,000 troops. Part of the reason for this campaign was to gain raw materials, especially iron ore, and ports for the Navy to use to gain better access to the Atlantic Ocean. The campaign in Norway, which ended on 9 May, was considered successful, but had the negative affect of costing Germany a large portion of her surface fleet, which would have consequences later on that summer and fall.

On 10 May 1940 Germany unleashed Operation Yellow, the invasion of the Low Countries and France. This campaign saw the successful use of German airborne forces to capture specific strong points to include Eban Emael in Belgium. By the end of the invasion of France, Germany occupied Europe from the Atlantic coast of France up to

Norway, and east to the border of the Soviet Union. It was towards the end of the campaign in France that Italy declared war on Great Britain and France. Hitler attempted to persuade Italy not to enter the war at this point, saying it was unnecessary. Even though Italy did enter the war Hitler was still satisfied to allow Mussolini to deal with events in the Mediterranean situation as he saw fit, but as time went on the senior German leaders saw that the estimates made before the war about Italian capabilities were coming true. By the end of 1940 they realized that Italy would not be able to support its own forces.

Following the Battle for France, as the Allies knew Operation Yellow, Hitler decided to invade Great Britain and defeat the last remaining enemy in the west before turning his attention to the Soviet Union in the East. However, prior to invading England it was necessary to gain air superiority over the skies of Britain. Thus began the Battle of Britain, the German operation that lasted formally from July through September 1940. This battle was intended as the prelude for Operation Sealion, the sea-borne invasion of Britain, but because of the large losses of German aircraft and pilots the invasion of Britain never took place, however air attacks against Britain continued.

With the invasion of Great Britain cancelled, Germany was able to focus entirely on the invasion of the Soviet Union, which was scheduled for spring 1941. However, Italy threw a wrench into those plans. With the Italian debacle in Greece and the subsequent British occupation of Crete and Limnos in the Mediterranean, Germany was forced to plan an invasion of Greece in order to support her ally and throw the British out of the Balkans. At a conference on 4 November 1940, when Hitler announced his decision to occupy Gibraltar, the Balkans was brought sharply to the attention of Hitler and of the Army High Command because of the need to secure bases to launch the invasion of the Soviet Union and the need to secure necessary raw materials such as oil from Romania. Along with planning for the capture of Gibraltar to help close the Mediterranean to the British, the Führer also ordered that the Romanian oilfields be protected. He requested that plans should be drawn up for an invasion of Greece to be undertaken from the German bases in Romania and Bulgaria (code-named Marita) so as to enable the Luftwaffe to attack targets in the eastern Mediterranean, especially, Crete and Limnos.[9] Through the winter of 1940-1941 Germany used the four areas of national power of the DIME model--Diplomacy, Information, Military, and Economy--to get the Balkan countries of Hungary, Romania, Bulgaria, and Yugoslavia to sign the Tripartite Pact and become allies of Germany, thus allowing German forces to move freely through them in order to invade Greece. Germany was able to secure the signing of the pact and the support of all the countries, except Yugoslavia, where a coup occurred just prior to the signing of the pact and the new government decided not to sign. This action infuriated Hitler and caused him to require the invasion of Yugoslavia to punish the Yugoslavs for their actions. On 6 April 1941 air attacks against Belgrade signaled the beginning of Operation 25, the German invasion of Yugoslavia. By 13 April the capital of Belgrade was captured, and by 15 April Sarajevo was in German hands. On 6 April German forces in Bulgaria invaded Greece. Although the Metaxas Line, fortresses on the Greek-Bulgarian border, stopped the Germans until Yugoslavia fell on 17 April, by 27 April the whole Peloponnesian peninsula was overrun and Athens was in German control.[10]

In addition, while the Balkan campaign was in progress, Section L, the Operations Section of OKW, had to produce an appreciation to show whether it was more important for future strategy in the Mediterranean to occupy Crete or Malta. All officers of the section, whether from the Army, Navy, or Air Force, together with General Walter Warlimont, voted unanimously for the capture of Malta since it seemed to be the only way to secure permanently the sea-route to North Africa. Their views were, however, overtaken by events even before they reached General Alfred Jodl. Hitler was determined that Crete should not remain in the hands of the British because of the danger of air attacks on the Rumanian oilfields and he had further agreed with the Luftwaffe that from a base in Crete there were far reaching possibilities for offensive action in the eastern Mediterranean. A curious incident occurred in the connection of comparing Malta to Crete in 1941; shortly after the decision to invade Crete was made Hitler's senior aide, Colonel Schmundt, appeared in the OKW Section L offices and demanded that no mention should be made in Section L's war diary of these differences of opinion within supreme Headquarters or of any similar cases which might occur in the future.[11] The details of the invasion will be discussed in the next chapter, but briefly the invasion was conducted from 20 May through 1 June. It was a successful operation, but like Norway incurred losses in specific areas that would affect operations in the future.

While the planning for the Balkans campaign was ongoing, Germany was also beginning operations in North Africa to support the collapsing Italian Army. In January 1941 X Fliegerkorps was sent to Sicily to assist in reopening the strangled Italian supply lines to North Africa by neutralizing the airpower and sea power exerted by the British from Malta, this was but a minor diversion to German planning.[12] In February 1941 Hitler sent General Erwin Rommel and the Deutsches Afrika Korps (DAK). Rommel managed to push back the British forces and get as far as the Egyptian frontier, but they were unable to capture the city of Tobruk. A siege to capture the port city would continue on and off until the next summer. The campaign through North Africa would be the reason why Malta became a focal point for all forces. In the end North Africa would be an area of good news through 1941 when the upcoming Russian campaign began to have setbacks.

As the culmination of German planning, Operation Barbarossa began on 22 June 1941. The German campaign in the Soviet Union would become the main effort of German strategic and operational planning for the rest of the war. From the time it started through the opening of the second front in France in 1944, all other areas would play a supporting role to the fighting that took place all through the Eastern Front. By the end of 1941 German forces had come within sight of Moscow, only to be pushed back by strong Soviet forces on 6 December 1941. As the year ended German forces had gone onto the defensive through the bitter Russian winter.

Because the senior command elements of the German armed forces were far more preoccupied with global events--and in particular the titanic struggle with the Soviet Union--than to be continually concerned with Middle East affairs. This was the task delegated to GeneralFeldmarschall Albert Kesselring who was appointed OB South on 28 November 1941. From his office in Rome he commanded all German land and air forces in the Mediterranean theater, but was subordinate to the Italian Chief of Staff.[13]

Italy

Italy was by far the least prepared of the three countries when it entered the war in 1940. It had difficulty defeating far less capable nations much less acting as an aggressor nation against France and Great Britain. This section will discuss not only Italian strategic operations through 1941, but also what led the Italians to war and the state of their armed forces when the war began in order to give a more complete picture of Italy's readiness for war.

Benito Mussolini had been the fascist leader of Italy since 1922 and by 1940 occupied no less then five high offices within the Italian government to include Supreme Commander and head of the Government, Minister of War, Minister for the Navy, and Minister for the Air Force. He was also the Minister of the Interior and President of the Fascist Grand Council and was the sole advocate for entering the war in 1940.[15]

Italy entered into the "Pact of Steel" with Germany on 22 May 1939. The pact was the Italian-German alliance and was signed by the two foreign ministers, Galeazzo Ciano of Italy and Joachim von Ribbentrop of Germany. The treaty consisted of seven Articles which maybe summarized as follows: Article I: the two nations would remain in continuous contact with each other in order to be in agreement on matters in Europe. Article II: The two nations would consult with each other on matters of mutual interest and if one nation's security were threatened then the other would offer its diplomatic and military support. Article III: If one of the countries were attacked then the other nation would come to its aid with all its military might on land, sea, and air. Article IV: The two countries were to "further intensify their collaboration in the military field, and in the field of war economy." Article V: If in a war together, neither nation would seek peace without the agreement of the other. Article VI: The nations understood the need for an alliance and would continue to work in the future to "promote the adequate development of the common interests" between the two nations. Article VII: The agreement would be valid for ten years and would be renewed prior to the end of the ten-year period.[14] Italy had more to gain from the Pact then Germany did, even though leading up to the signing of the pact both Hitler and Mussolini were on approximately equal footing on the strategic stage. However, Italy was far behind Germany in the economic and military arenas.

As a member of the "Pact of Steel" with Germany, Italy was under some obligations to assist Germany if Germany was attacked; however, since Germany was not attacked when she invaded Poland in 1939, Mussolini saw no need to enter the war to assist Germany. By 1940 Italy had expanded her empire to include the areas of Ethiopia, Libya, and Albania. Through the first few months of 1940 Italy had no intention of entering the war, but that did not prevent Mussolini from preparing for eventually entering the war as Hitler's ally. In a letter to Hitler in early 1940 Mussolini claimed that Italy was not prepared to enter the war soon and that he wanted to wait until Italy would "not be a burden but a relief to you," however, he stated that he was "accelerating the tempo of military preparations."[16] This changed by the end of March when Mussolini decided to shift from "non-belligerent" to combatant, although he had not selected the date to officially enter the war.[17] Up to this point Italy's stance of non-belligerence relieved Germany of the need to support her Latin neighbor with scarce war supplies. This stance also proved to be helpful to the Western Allies who were able to focus their supplies and personnel to other theaters of war, specifically to defending France and attempting to defeat the German invasion of Norway.[18]

When Mussolini informed his senior leadership about entering the war, they were all against such action. Marshal Badoglio spoke for the majority of Mussolini's advisors when he told the Duce that Italy was unprepared for war. No raw materials had been stockpiled and what reserves were on hand would soon be exhausted. Italy's industrial base was only one-tenth of Germany's and even with supplies was not organized to provide the equipment needed to fight a modern war of long duration.[19] The Italian Supreme Defense Committee met under Mussolini's chairmanship in February 1940. Each of the three service Chiefs of Staff presented a report on the rearmament programs drawn up and what actual work was going forward. The minister of Foreign Exchange and Currencies, Raffaello Riccardi, threw cold water on the entire rearmament program by pointing out that Italy's limited reserves in gold and foreign currencies made it impossible to implement such ambitious plans. Raw materials essential to conducting a war economy were lacking. He concluded his grim assessment by demanding a revision of the rearmament program that reflected Italy's actual economic condition.[20] Despite all the recommendations from his advisors Mussolini still decided to push forward to enter the war.

While the senior leadership of Italy was trying to give Mussolini an accurate picture and attempting to dissuade him from plunging Italy into war with the western powers, Germany was also trying to the same thing. The Germans had long been aware of Italy's military and economic weakness. In April 1938, the German Naval High Command (OKM) reported to the Armed Forces Command (OKW):

> In our opinion, in a war with England, Italy, as an ally, would be a burden of the first order, especially in regards to the war's economic prosecution; while Italy would not be able to provide effective military support in districts of strategic importance to Germany (except in the Mediterranean). On this basis, OKM recommends that Italy for the time being (if war breaks out) act as a benevolent neutral.[21]

On 10 March 1940, German Foreign Minister von Ribbentrop visited Rome and informed his hosts that Germany was going to attack the West and had over 200 highly equipped divisions assigned for this assault. Eight days later, Mussolini met Hitler at the Brenner Pass. Hitler said that the war would be over that summer and Italy's military involvement was not required. It was up to Mussolini to decide if and when Italy entered the war.[22] Because the Italians were not prepared for war, the Germans actually tried to do everything possible to prevent their ally from entering the war.

When Germany was preparing for the invasion of Poland in August of 1939, Italian participation in the war had been expected by the Germans under provisions of the "Pact of Steel". However, by June 1940 it was clear to many in Hitler's circle that Italy would prove to be a needless complication, if not an actual hindrance to their war effort. The French were close to defeat and Italian involvement at this point might well interfere with military operations and the post-war peace negotiations. On 2 June 1940, Mussolini sent a brief message to Hitler, in which he revealed his timetable. On Monday, 10 June, he would declare was against Britain and France. The next morning military operations would commence. Right up to the last minute, the Germans tried to persuade Mussolini to at least delay his entry into the war.[23] Further confirmation was given to the Germans, if they needed any, through the Italian leadership of Italy's fundamental unpreparedness for war; they received it from Marshal Badoglio, the Chief of Commando Supremo. On 5 June 1940, the German Embassy in Rome telegraphed a message marked "MOST URGENT" to Berlin, in which the German Military Attaché, General Enno von Rintelen, reported that Badoglio had confided, "We could not expect a great deal from the Italian armed forces since the Army and Air Force were not ready and there was a long frontier to be protected. He hoped that the war would be brought to an end with the same speed with which we had conducted the first phase.[24]

Now that we have seen what the leadership tried to do to prevent Mussolini from dragging Italy into the war let us take a specific look at the Italian armed forces and actually how prepared each was for a major war. Up to this point all the military operations that Italy had conducted were against what would be considered third world countries, specifically, Ethiopia and Albania, but fighting against Great Britain and France would be far different.

The Italian armed forces were organized into three service commands, the Army, Air Force, and Navy. They were theoretically co-equal but subordinated to the Supreme Command, which tended to be dominated by the Army. Of the three services, the Army, the Regio Esercito, was in the worst shape at the outbreak of the war.[25] Numerically, the Italians had a vast advantage against the British. The Italian Army then numbered about 86 divisions.[26] In Ethiopia and Eritrea, some 200,000 Italian and colonial troops under the Duke of Aosta faced 18,000 British and assorted Empire forces, equally divided in Kenya and the Sudan. In North Africa, Marshal Graziani, who took command in late June after Marshal Balbo was killed by "friendly" antiaircraft fire, had nearly 250,000 troops at his disposal. General Archibald Wavell, the Commander in Chief, Middle East, since July 1939, had only 36,000 British, Indian, and New Zealand troops with which to hold Egypt.[27] This numerical superiority was misleading when compared to the shortcomings in the areas of supply and the fact that most of the armaments used by the Italian Army were outdated, and it was estimated that the ability to upgrade and refurbish the Army would not be completed within the next five years. The Italian Army also had a drastic shortage of motorized vehicles and modern tanks.[28]

Like the Army, the Italian Air Force, Regia Aeronautica, was a quality force in numbers alone. By 1935, the Regia Aeronautica held many of the world's records for aircraft performance. However, it came to suffer from bloc obsolescence and by 1940 was rather closer to the level of a Balkan air force, such as Yugoslavia or Bulgaria.[29] A Luftwaffe intelligence report had said of the Regia Aeronautica, "On the basis of their backward tactics, Italian air units will suffer setbacks at the beginning of a war against an opponent with strong fighter and air defense. It is questionable, considering the Italian mentality, whether the Italian Air force possesses the inner strength to overcome such weaknesses."[30] In broad terms the Italian Air Force was numerically superior to those elements of the RAF that opposed it in the Middle East area generally and over the Mediterranean in particular. The Italians had some 2,600 first line aircraft.[31] Mussolini had taken great pains to create a large, modern air force when he came into power. He once boasted that he would black out the sun with his planes. To be fair, the Regia Aeronautica probably reached its peak in 1936. After this time its war potential was reduced through lack of reserves and equipment.[32]

Of the three services, the Navy, the Regia Marina, was in the best condition to fight. In 1922, when Mussolini assumed power, the Italian Navy was in very poor condition, with four battleships, seven antiquated cruisers taken over from the Austro-Hungarian and German navies at the end of World War I, and a relative handful of old destroyers, torpedo boats, and service ships. As a signatory to the Washington Naval Treaty of 1922 and later the London Naval Treaty of 1930 the Italians were limited on the ability to expand the Navy.[33] However, by 1940 the Italians had six battleships, including two new ones of 35,000 tons; seven 10,000-ton heavy cruisers; 21 light cruisers; 67

destroyers; 69 torpedo boats; 117 submarines; and mine-sweepers, repair ships, and special assault craft *(MAS-mezzi d' assaulto)*. However, the Italian Navy was less than it appeared on paper. Apart from a few minor engagements in the Adriatic, the Italian Navy saw little action in World War I, nor did it carry out much training during the inter-war years, so it lacked the experience in naval strategy and tactics necessary to fight a prominent sea power like Great Britain. In 1939, for example, it had four old World War I battleships, built in 1911 in service, only two of which (*Cavour* and *Cesare*) had been refitted and modernized. In 1940 the fleet was considerably improved by its commissioning of two new "fast" battleships, the 35,000-ton *Littorio* (name changed to Italia in August 1943) and *Vittorio Veneto*. Italy had no aircraft carriers, arguing that its land-based aircraft were always in range. However, this would prove to be a decided disadvantage. It was the large Italian submarine fleet that seemed to pose the greatest danger when war was declared, as four-fifths of them were ready for action. The British opinion of the Italian Navy is explained in a war time HMSO booklet entitled East of Suez, West of Malta and published in 1943. In it the Admiralty says:

> Although Italian seamen have never lacked courage, her Navy has not the professional and psychological outlook of the blue-water sailor; and under Mussolini's regime, political uncertainty must inevitably have penetrated the wardrooms and mess-decks of the fleet. When that happened, it was perhaps no longer completely reliable as a weapon of war. A suspicion of this may have decided Italy to put her faith in air power and take no undue risks with the fleet.[37]

As an aspect of the Navy, little consideration was taken for the Italian merchant shipping when the war began, specifically where all the ships were located in the world. In 1940 Italy had 786 ships over 500 gross tons. When Mussolini had declared war, one-third of them, totaling nearly 1,200,000 gross tons, had been sailing outside the Mediterranean and had not been withdrawn to safe waters before the declaration. As a consequence, many of them were lost at the very outset of hostilities. Many of the ships caught overseas in June 1940 were among Italy's best. Of the 500 ships remaining under Italian control after the war began, many were unsuited for war service, either because of their large size, as with the ocean liners pressed into service, their age, slow speed, or limited size. This situation was to have an immediate impact on resupplying North Africa while fighting the Royal Navy and Royal Air Force to get the convoys to their objective.[38]

Now that we have a better picture of the Italian armed forces let us take a look at what their instructions were when Mussolini declared war. With the outbreak of hostilities, Commando Supremo issued plans that directed the armed forces to conduct the following operations:

> Land fronts: offensive in the Western Alps against France (which was at the point of seeking an armistice with Germany);
> Precautionary observation of Yugoslavia;
> Initial defensive attitude on the Albania front: same to be modified in accordance with developments in the situation in the Balkans; Defensive in Libya, on the Tunisian as well as on the Egyptian front;
> Defensive in the Aegean;
> Air-sea offensive throughout the Mediterranean.[39]

Mussolini had told Hitler that military operations would commence the day following his declaration of war. That next morning, 11 June 1940, elements of the Italian Air Force began bombing Malta. At the same time Italy began offensive operations against the French along their mutual border. The purpose for these operations and the basic reason for Italy entering the war in the first place was so Mussolini could have a legitimate seat at the peace negotiations when the German campaign ended in France. However, despite France's poor showing against the Wehrmacht in the north, the French were not only able to hold against the Italians, but were actually able to take counter-offensive action of their own and beat back the Italians prior to surrendering to the Germans. This was the first setback for Italy and for Mussolini's prestige as a political leader.

The next setback for Italy came in North Africa where Italy held Libya and Ethiopia. Between these two areas were approximately 250,000 troops facing 40,000 British and Dominion forces in Egypt. The Italians under Marshal d'Armata Rodolfo Graziani invaded and occupied British Somaliland on 17 August 1940, possibly cutting off the merchant transit route through the Red Sea and cutting of the British route from India. On 13 September Graziani reluctantly invaded Egypt under pressure from Mussolini. The assault into Egypt was initially successful. The Italians were able to capture Sidi Barrani, 65 miles inside Egypt's border with Libya; however British General Wavell sent an attack force of 30,000 troops to recapture Sidi Barrani, which they did, along with 20,000 Italian prisoners. By the end of the British campaign, which started on 9 December 1940, the British had beaten the Italians back across Libya to Tripoli, and had captured the port of Tobruk and more than 130,000 Italian prisoners.[40]

While fighting was going on in North Africa Mussolini felt it necessary, at the end of September, to order the demobilization of 600,000 troops, over half of the Army, because he could not afford to maintain them over the winter. At the same time as fighting in North Africa and ordering a demobilization Mussolini planned for the invasion of Greece, which began prior to the beginning of November 1940. Greece and the Balkans was an area that Germany had long attempted to prevent Italy from invading. Since mid-summer, the Germans had been warning Mussolini not to extend the war into the Balkans because Germany needed this region to be secured prior to invading the

Soviet Union in 1941. On the morning of 28 October 1940, ten weak Italian divisions invaded Greece through the mountains of Albania. Prior to the invasion Mussolini told Ciano, "Hitler keeps confronting me with accomplished facts. This time I am going to pay him back in his own coin. He will find out from the papers that I have occupied Greece."[41] The Italian attack was one of the most ill prepared operations of the Second World War. By November 1, the doughty Greeks counter-attacked and forced the hapless Italians back toward Albania. So serious was the Greek threat to Albania that Mussolini was forced to pour men and equipment into that front. The Navy had to divert traffic from the North African supply route to Albania. The Italian Air Force ended up sending over 650 aircraft to support operations in the Balkans.[42] With the Italians on the defensive in North Africa and now Greece, it became more publicly evident to Italy's ally, Germany that the Italians would require more and more assistance from Germany in order to survive in the war.

Throughout 1941 Italy was unable to conduct any offensive campaigns on its own. German troops backed up the Italian troops in North Africa, while in the Balkans the Italians were kept on the defensive by the Greeks even though in April 1941 Greece was invaded by Germany. Only when Germany defeated Greece did the offensive action against Italian forces in Albania end. With the German invasion of Russia in June 1941, Mussolini did commit several divisions to Operation Barbarossa. The horrific Italian losses on the Eastern Front further eroded Mussolini's support with the King and the Italian people.[43]

Through all these campaigns Malta still remained in British possession. There were leaders on both sides that wondered why the Italians never captured the island at the outset of the war. In fact Hitler was vexed that Mussolini had failed to capture Malta at the very outset of war.[44]

While discussing the strategic picture of the Mediterranean in 1941 particular attention needs to be given the operation that concluded the German invasion of the Balkans. This was an operation that would have a direct impact on future operations against Malta and mark the final major use of one of Germany's elite Fallschirmjäger.

---

[1]Jason McDonald, *The World War II Multimedia Database* [database on-line]; available from http://www.worldwar2database.com/html/france.htm; Internet; accessed on December 2005 (hereafter cited McDonald, http://www.worldwar2database.com/html/_____.htm).

[2]*Wikipedia: The Free Encyclopedia* [database on-line]; available from http://en.wikipedia.org/wiki/Battle_of_Dunkirk; Internet; accessed on February 2006 (hereafter cited Wikipedia, http://en.wikipedia.org/wiki/_____).

[3]Lutton, 33.

[4]Ibid., 27.

[5]McDonald, http://www.worldwar2database.com/html/africa.htm.

[6]McDonald, http://www.worldwar2database.com/html/uk.htm.

[7]Ibid.

[8]Forty, 22.

[9]Matthew Cooper *The German Army 1933-1945: Its Political and Military Failure.* (Chelsea, Michigan: Scarborough House, 1990), 251.

[10]McDonald, http://www.worldwar2database.com/html/greece.htm.

[11]Walter Warlimont, *Inside Hitler's Headquarters 1939-1945,* (Novato, California: Presidio Press, 1964), 131.

[12]Kenneth Macksey, *Kesselring, German Master Strategist of The Second World War.* (London, England: Greenhill Books, 1996), 105.

[13]Forty, 48.

[15]Forty, 43.

[14]Adolf Hitler.ws: An Apolitical Historical Website, [database on-line]; available from http://www.adolfhitler.ws/lib/proc/pactofsteel.html, Internet; accessed on February 2006.

[16]Lutton, 6.

[17]Ibid., 8.

[18]Ibid., 4.

[19]Gerhard Schreiber; Bernd Stegmann; and Detlaf Vogel, *Germany and the Second World War,* vol 3 *The Mediterranean, South-east Europe, and North Africa 1939-1941.* (Oxford, England: Clarendon Press, 1995), 25.

[20]Lutton, 7.

[21]Ibid., 12.

[22]Ibid., 8.

[23]Ibid., 12-13.

[24]Ibid., 14.

[25]Ibid., 16.

[26]Forty, 21-22.

[27]Lutton, 25.

[28]Schreiber, Stegmann, and Vogel, 66-67.

[29]Lutton, 17-18.

[30]Ibid., 13.

[31]Forty, 46.

[32]Ibid., 21.

[33]Wikipedia, http://en.wikipedia.org/wiki/London_Naval_Treaty.

[37]Forty, 43-46.

[38]Lutton, 135.

[39]Ibid., 22.

[40]McDonald, http://www.worldwar2database.com/html/africa.htm.

[41]Lutton, 45.

[42]Ibid., 41-45.

[43]McDonald, http://www.worldwar2database.com/html/italy.htm.

[44]Lutton, 23.

CHAPTER 3

OPERATION MERCURY (INVASION OF CRETE)

Now that the strategic stage has been set it is important to examine the one operation that would be looked upon during the planning for the invasion of Malta, Operation Mercury, the codename for the airborne invasion of Crete in May 1941. The ten-day battle at the end of May 1941 was the largest use of airborne forces up to that time. It was the first time that almost an entire division was dropped onto an objective and used to secure a major strategic target.[1]

Location and Topography

As the fourth largest island in the Mediterranean, the island of Crete dominates the entrance into the Aegean Sea and the southern approaches to the Turkish Straits. It is located just sixty miles south of the Greek mainland in the eastern Mediterranean, 460 miles from Egypt, 240 miles from Libya, and 600 miles from the Suez Canal. This location had strategic implications for both Germany and Great Britain in 1941.[2] Crete is approximately 160 miles long from west to east and varies in width from 8 to 35 miles. The interior of the island is covered by mountains that rise in the western part of the island to an elevation of 8,100 feet. The southern coast is covered with cliffs, so that the only usable port along this part of the coast is the small harbor of Sphakia. There are only a few north-south roads, and the only motor road to Sphakia, ends 1,300 feet above the town. The sole major traffic artery runs close to the northern coast and connects the towns of Maleme and Canea in the west, and Retimo and Heraklion as you move east. Suda Bay is located on the northern coast and lies between Canea and Retimo, on the western half of the island. The topography of the island therefore favored the invader, since the mountainous terrain left no other alternative to the British but to construct their airfields close to the exposed northern coast.[3]

Operational Situation

At the beginning of 1940 Crete was not occupied by any of the warring powers. Even after Italy declared war no one occupied the island. It was only after the Italian surprise attack on Greece in October 1940 that the British occupied Crete with one brigade in addition to some Greek units. The British improved the three local airfields at Maleme, Retimo, and Heriklion and the harbor installations at Suda Bay, where they established a naval refueling base.[4] In November 1940 when the British landed their first element of troops, General Sir Archibald Wavell, British Commander of Middle East Command, considered Crete as a secondary priority. Wavell's command was overstretched in accomplishing its priorities with the Italians in North Africa and Greece, unrest in Syria and Iraq. Even though his forces were busy this did not mean that Crete as a military garrison should be entirely neglected.[5] During the German invasion of Greece, Crete was first used as the main supply base for British operations in the Balkans and later as the collection point for most of the troops evacuated from Greece. Once the evacuation of Greece was complete there were 32,000 British and Imperial troops and 14,000 Greek troops on Crete. The original garrison, numbering approximately 5,000 men, was fully equipped, but the majority of the troops evacuated from Greece arrived tired, disorganized, and equipped only with the small arms they saved during the withdrawal.[6]

The British had always regarded the Mediterranean as a bridge and not as a dividing line and therefore they expected that the Luftwaffe would bypass Crete to pose a real threat against the British fleet in Alexandria and British bases in the central and eastern Mediterranean, such as Malta and Gibraltar. The views of the US Navy were even more extreme, but saw the possibility of Germany capturing Crete. The US Navy visualized that with the German occupation of Crete; the British fleet would be driven from the Mediterranean and even considered an end to the war to be possible.[7] In view of the massive strength of the Luftwaffe in the Balkans, General Sir Archibald Wavell argued that Crete could not be held against a determined attack. Despite this assertion Prime Minister Churchill did not order its evacuation, but instead put General Sir Bernard Freyberg, Commanding General of the New Zealand Division, in charge of Crete's defense.[8]

For the Germans, possession of Crete would secure the Aegean Sea for Axis shipping and provide air bases to launch offensives against British forces in Egypt, and in Hitler's opinion lessen Britain's influence in the Eastern Mediterranean. The Balkan region, as well as Crete, was also important to Germany as Hitler set his sights on the Soviet Union. Control of the Balkans would provide a secure right flank for his invading forces and protect the oilfields in Romania, which provided necessary fuel for his war machine. Allied control of Crete with their air and sea superiority would deny the Germans a strategic military foothold in the region.[9] As long as the British held the island, they would be able to maintain naval and air superiority in the eastern Mediterranean; Crete could serve as a springboard for British landings along the Balkan coast; and it was a potential air base from which the Romanian oil fields could be attacked.[10] It is important to note that General Erwin Rommel's Afrika Korps was beginning its initial offensive against the British forces in North Africa concurrently with the German offensive on the Balkan Peninsula. Its initial operations held and then drove General Wavell's army back towards the Egyptian frontier. This defeat was brought about as a result of Churchill's order to Wavell to use part of the 8th Army as an expeditionary force to Greece.[11] Keeping the sea-lanes of communication open to German forces in North Africa became paramount to prevent failure there.

As the conclusion to the campaign in Greece was in sight by mid April 1941 the focus moved to invading a strategic island in the Mediterranean that could influence future operations in the Mediterranean and North Africa and protect Germany's strategic interests. The German senior leadership was split as to whether to invade Malta or Crete. On 15 April General der Flieger Kurt Student, one of General der Flieger Alexander Löhr's subordinates and commander of XI Flieger Corps, submitted to Göring a plan for capturing Crete. On the same day the Army High Command, Ober Kommando der Heeres (OKH), transmitted a plan for the invasion of Malta. The latter plan had been under consideration for some time.[12] Speaking for the OKW Operations Staff, General Alfred Jodl recommended that they seize Malta. It had been less than a week since an entire convoy bound for North Africa had been sunk and it was the opinion of Jodl's staff that the over-all situation would be helped the most by capturing the British island base. The capture of Malta would eliminate the threat to the Africa-bound convoys, which the capture of Crete did not offer this advantage. The OKW operations staff foresaw that the onset of the Russian campaign would lead to a relative reduction in German air strength in the Mediterranean and that support of Rommel's forces would be the top priority. Neutralizing Malta dropped to the third priority for the Luftwaffe.[13]

During the debate over invading Malta or Crete, Hitler decided that Crete was more important and selected an invasion there over an attack on the island of Malta, even though Malta was a British stronghold and was influencing Axis operations in North Africa. In Hitler's opinion, Crete with its potential for larger airfields and good anchorage was more important then Malta.[14] Capturing Crete would also push British bombers back to Egypt and out of range of the Romanian oil fields at Ploesti.

On 20 April, after a conference with General Student, Hitler decided in favor of invading Crete rather than Malta, and five days later Directive No.28 was issued under the code designation Operation Mercury.[15] The majority of senior leaders believed that Malta was a more important target and needed to be eliminated. However, giving Malta priority over Crete would have done more to eliminate a threat to German offensive operations in North Africa. It also would have required commitment of substantial German resources to a potentially costly undertaking, which would have had to be planned and implemented, from the outset, with an already unreliable ally instead of using only German troops as in Crete.[16]

So Hitler decided to give priority to the assault on Crete. In his opinion, the possession of Crete, allowed the Luftwaffe to cover the Eastern Mediterranean and bring Alexandria and the Suez Canal within operational range, thus jeopardizing Malta's resupply from the east, and sharply diminishing its value as a stepping-stone for staging area for eastbound resupply operations. Operation Mercury could be initially mounted on an independent basis, bringing the Italians in later, if at all. Most importantly, it might make the invasion of Malta unnecessary.[17] According to this directive the necessary preparations were to be made to invade and occupy Crete. It was to serve as a base for future air operations against the British in the eastern Mediterranean. At the time ample ground forces were available in the southern Balkans, but a major obstacle stood in the path of the seizure of Crete. British naval superiority in the eastern Mediterranean remained uncontested and a sea-borne landing in Crete could not be affected until the British fleet had been destroyed or at least driven out of the Aegean.[18]

Planning

With the issuing of War directive No. 28, preparations for the invasion of Crete began; however, it took time to assemble the necessary men and equipment since they were scattered all across Europe. As a result, D-Day for Operation Mercury was put back until 20 May. This delay allowed the confused defense of Crete to be put into some sort of order.[19] General der Flieger Alexander Löhr, the commander of IV Luftflotte, was put in charge of executing Operation Mercury. His task force consisted of the following units:

1. VIII Fliegerkorps under the command of General der Flieger Freiherr (Baron) Wolfram von Richthofen.
2. XI Fliegerkorps, commanded by Generalmajor Kurt Student: 10 air transport groups with approximately 600 troop carriers and 100 gliders; one reconnaissance squadron; the reinforced 7th Flieger (Airborne) Division; 5th Gebirgs (Mountain) Division; one regiment of the 6th Gebirgs Division; several airborne antiaircraft, engineer, and medical battalions forming the corps troops. The total strength of the invasion force was approximately 25,000.
3. One Bombardment group, which was to lay mines in the Suez Canal area.
4. One naval patrol group and one air-sea rescue squadron.[20]

During the early planning process General Löhr favored a single concentrated drop to seize the airfield at Maleme, followed by a build up of additional infantry and heavy weapons, and then a conventional advance up the island from west to east. Such an approach would allow for a consolidated German effort and ease of command and control; however, it might allow the British time to reinforce the garrison either by sea, or by landing troops at either Heraklion or Retimo. Generalmajor Student suggested no less then seven separate drops, the most important being around the airfields at Maleme, Retimo and Heraklion, with the focus on Heraklion. Student's plan would enable the Germans to seize all the main strategic points at the outset. It was predicated on the ground resistance being minimal. In the end Göring imposed a compromise plan. The drops on D-Day by 15,000 combat troops of the 7th Flieger Division would be made in two waves: the first in the morning around the town of Hania and the airfield at Maleme, the second in the late afternoon against the airfields at Heraklion and Retimo. This would be followed on D+1 by the arrival of the 7,000 mountain troops of 5th Gebirgs Division under Generalmajor Julius Ringel and the sea-borne elements.[21]

Gruppe West, commanded by Generalmajor Eugen Meindl, consisted of the entire Luftlande Sturmregiment, minus two companies of glider troops that were attached to Gruppe Mitte, which would land in the first wave and had the objective of securing Maleme airfield. The divisional commander, Generalleutnant Wilhelm Süssman, commanded Gruppe Mitte. The first wave would consist of the divisional headquarters along with the two glider companies from the Luftlande Sturmregiment as well as Oberst Richard Heidrich's 3rd Fallschirmjäger Regiment (FJR), reinforced by engineer and AA units. Their objective would be to land in Prison Valley and attack towards Hania and

Suda. The second wave would be commanded by Oberst Alfred Sturm and consist of the 1st and 3rd Battalions, 2nd FJR, with the town of Retimo as its objective. Gruppe Ost, commanded by Oberst Bruno Bräuer and landing in the second wave, consisted of the 1st Fallschirmjäger Regiment, reinforced by the 2nd Battalion, 2nd (FJR) with Heraklion as its objective.[22]

Even though there was an initial disagreement about the plans, Göring's compromise plan was supported by all the planners. All the senior leaders including the Kriegsmarine's Konteradmiral Karl-Georg Schuster agreed that Maleme should be one of the main targets. It was the closest objective to the island's administrative center, Hania, and Suda Bay. It was also the shortest flight time from the Greek mainland. This latter aspect was important, as the 502 operational Ju-52s could not carry all the assault elements in a single drop; the maximum was around 6,000 in one lift. This meant that, even had the German intelligence estimates proved correct, the attacking forces would have been at a 1:2 disadvantage. This issue's impact will be further discussed below.[23]

There was no agreement between the three services on how to conduct the invasion or if it should be conducted. While the Luftwaffe approached the invasion of Crete with full confidence, the other two services maintained a reserved attitude. Unable to participate in the operation with its own ships, the German Navy was all the more skeptical because of the manifest weakness of the Italian Fleet. On the other hand, the German Navy welcomed this opportunity for the possible defeat of the British Mediterranean Fleet. The Navy was responsible for securing the sea-lanes and was to contact the Italian Navy to coordinate for this purpose as well as for the procurement of the necessary shipping space. The Army's lack of enthusiasm was based on the assumption that the British would defend Crete to the bitter end since it protected their flank in North Africa and at the Suez Canal. The Army was to provide suitable units to reinforce the airborne corps, including an armored combat team that was to be sea borne. Moreover, the Army was to make available the occupation forces, which would be needed to relieve the airborne troops once the seizure of the island had been accomplished. The Army also had reservations because there was a real danger that too many first-class troops might be diverted to a secondary theater of war while planning for Barbarossa was underway. In view of the impending invasion of Russia, such commitments had to be avoided if at all possible. The initial invasion would therefore have to be executed by airborne forces. Almost single-handed, the Luftwaffe would have to neutralize the enemy's air and ground defenses, airland and drop the German assault troops, defeat the British naval forces, and support the ground operations by airlifting supplies.[24]

Intelligence

German intelligence badly underestimated the Allied strength on the island. In all, the forces on the island numbered some 32,000 Commonwealth troops and 14,000 Greek soldiers. This was significantly more than the German intelligence estimate of some 10,000 Commonwealth troops and the remnants of ten Greek divisions. In fact the picture that British intelligence had of the German intentions was far better than the Germans information on Allied dispositions. From the end of April, a stream of 'Ultra' intelligence, decrypted by the code-breaking office at Bletchley Park, indicated that the Germans were planning to land an airborne invasion of Crete with emphasis being on the capture of the airfields, and then following that up with air landing some reinforcements, and bringing in others by sea. Additionally, it was very difficult for General Löhr to conceal the build-up of Luftflotte IV in Greece. This information was passed along to Freyberg, but its impact was diluted to protect the secret of the 'Ultra' breakthrough.[25]

Without knowing what information they were giving up, the Germans did everything possible to maintain operational security. However, the element of surprise--so important in any airborne operation--was not maintained. British agents in Greece transmitted accurate information on the German build up and left little doubt as to the next German objective. These troop and supply movements were unobserved. On the last few nights preceding D-day, the British bombed the assembly areas, but caused little damage.[26]

Logistics

Along with the difficulty of bringing the troops together on such little notice, the logistical problems compounded the planning. Every available means of transportation had to be used to move the airborne corps, including the 22nd Division, to its assembly areas, but these movements were not to interfere with the assembly of forces for operation Barbarossa.[27] The Greek railroads could not be repaired in time, and coastal shipping had to carry the main supply load. The 7th Flieger Division was moved by rail from Germany to Arad and Craiova in Romania and then by truck to Sofiya and Salonika to airfields in southern Greece. The mountain troops had participated in the Greek campaign and were given special training in airborne operations. The truck transportation available, including nonorganic transport columns provided by Twelfth Army, was very limited, and the situation was aggravated by the fact that supplies had to be transported from bases in Austria, Romania, and Bulgaria; and it is necessary to remember that the roads were in very poor condition and the difficult terrain in Greece also attributed to the transportation problems. Aviation gasoline was the biggest problem because the tanker fleet was too small, and some of the tankers that had formerly been available had been lost during the Balkan campaign. The shortage of gasoline gave rise to even more anxiety because an adequate supply was essential for an operation in which planes were the primary form of transportation for both troop and supply movements. The solution of the logistical problems caused some delay and resulted in the postponement of D-Day from 16 to 20 May.[28]

Operational

General Student, aware of the successes that the German Army was achieving in the Greek campaign, saw that this victory could be fully exploited if his 'island hopping' campaign was executed.[29] At H plus 8 hours the second wave was to jump over Retimo and Heraklion without the assistance of gliderborne forces. Each group was to consist of one parachute combat team composed of infantry, antiaircraft artillery, engineers, and medical personnel. The four groups, separated by distances varying between ten and seventy-five miles, were to establish contact at the earliest possible moment. On D plus 1 the mountain troops were to be airlifted to the three airfields, which would be cleared of enemy forces. The naval convoys would land at the same time at Suda Bay and any minor ports that would be open to shipping.

Student, commanding XI Fliegerkorps, was forced to work to a very tight deadline. He had only a few weeks in which to plan and carry out the operation, and the difficulties facing him and his staff officers were enormous. The first blow was that the 22nd Luftlande Division, part of the Corps establishment, would not be available for the operation. The substitute for the 22nd was the 5th Gebirgs Division—a crack unit and one competent to fight through the mountainous Cretan terrain—but a formation with absolutely no experience in air transport operations. Then, too, XI Fliegerkorps had too few aircraft to carry the para/gliderborne contingents in a single 'lift'. There would have to be two waves of drops; a shuttle service with all the disadvantages and delays of such an operation.[30] The assembly of all units that were to participate in Operation Mercury took place within a little less than two weeks.[31]

As the Germans put their invasion plan together in a few short weeks, the Allies had six months to prepare Crete for invasion from either the air or by sea.[32] The British expected an attack on Crete. Their countermeasures were based on the assumption that an airborne invasion could not succeed without the landing of heavy weapons, reinforcements, and supplies by sea. By intercepting these supplies with the Royal Navy, the British hoped to be able to decide the issue in their favor.[33]

The belief that Crete would be attacked did not push the British leaders in the Mediterranean to prepare properly for an attack. Despite Winston Churchill's belief that Crete was strategically important in October 1940, Middle East Command Headquarters did not produce a general plan for defense and evacuation of the island should it come under attack. During the six months that Great Britain occupied Crete prior to the invasion, there were seven commanders. This showed a lack of priority for Crete from Middle East Command Headquarters. The first commander of the island was British Brigadier O.H. Tidbury. He was given a clear mission to defend Suda Bay and prevent and defeat enemy forces from occupying the island. General Tidbury accurately predicted the German airborne assault locations at Maleme, Retimo, and Heraklion, with the main effort at Suda Bay. He also assumed that there would be other landings at Retimo and Heraklion airstrips. With Tidbury in command of the island, there was great potential to develop his vision of defense into a bona fide ground defense plan. Unfortunately, resources were scarce and Wavell replaced Tidbury two months later in January 1941. Future commanders did not possess the same vision and urgency. The commanders after Tidbury did not establish and implement a defensive plan. Instead, their goal was to establish an administrative infrastructure necessary to support a large military garrison. Succeeding commanders were not in charge long enough to make significant changes to the garrison forming on Crete or to solidify defensive plans. Finally with the evacuation of Greece General Freyberg was placed in command of all allied forces on the island.[34]

On Crete General Freyberg identified five main objectives to defend: the airfields at Maleme, Retimo, and Heraklion, the administrative center of Hania and the port at Suda. While his assessments of the nature of the coming assault, its timing and targets was generally good, Freyberg's options were limited. Due to the security restrictions surrounding the decoded transcripts of German "Enigma" transmissions, it was difficult for him to be confident of the quality of the intelligence he received. The information received was not always complete, however, when a report that the 5th Gebirgs Division had been attached to the XI Fliegerkorps in addition to the 22nd Luftlande Division and that the Italian Navy would provide proper support this caused the seaborne force to be larger then the airborne force. This appraisal influenced General Freyberg to concentrate more on the seaborne rather then the airborne threat.[35] Even though he weighed more against a seaborne invasion General Freyberg disposed his ground forces with a view to preventing airborne landings on the airfields at Maleme, Retimo, and Heraklion and seaborne landings in Suda Bay and along the adjacent beaches. He divided his forces into four self-supporting groups split between objectives, the strongest of which was assigned to the defense of the vital Maleme airfield.[36]

A lack of transportation made it impossible to organize a mobile reserve force. Along with the transportation problem the garrison also suffered from poor communications and a lack of heavy weapons.[37] The armor available to the allies consisted of eight medium and sixteen light tanks and a few personnel carriers, which were divided equally among the four groups formed in the vicinity of the airfields near Canea. The artillery support was composed of some captured Italian guns with a limited supply of ammunition, ten 3.7-inch howitzers, and a few anti-aircraft batteries. The construction of fortifications had not been intensified until the Greek campaign had taken a turn for the worse. Therefore when the likelihood of an invasion against Crete became a strong probability the defenses were far from adequate or complete.[38]

There was little prospect of effective air cover and no one was sure if the Royal Navy could intervene in any meaningful way in the event of a seaborne threat.[39] The British naval forces defending Crete were based in Suda Bay, where the port installations were under constant German air observation. During the period immediately preceding the invasion intensive air attacks restricted the unloading of supplies to the hours from 2300 to 0330. Likewise, the British air bases in Egypt were too remote to provide adequate protection and logistical support for the forces defending Crete.[40]

The Allied commanders were handed an excellent picture of the pending invasion when a German Bf 110 crashed in Suda Bay and a map case and operational order for the 3rd Fallschirmjäger Regiment along with a summary of the entire operation were discovered by the Greeks and turned over to the British commanders. However, the British considered this a ruse even though it confirmed their own intelligence. Freyberg continued to focus more on the probability of a seaborne instead of an airborne assault. There was only a small allied reserve in the event that the Germans captured an airfield. The scene was set therefore for one of the most daring uses of airborne forces in history, the German attackers with a dreadfully inadequate picture of their target and enemy and the Allies effectively looking in the wrong direction.[41]

Operation Mercury finally took place from 20 May to 1 June 1941. At the end of the operation the German forces were able to secure the island and force the evacuation of a large portion of the allied forces with the remainder becoming prisoners of war. For the purposes of this thesis it is not important to recount the tactical fight for Crete; however there are a few operational items that need to be covered under the lessons learned because they would have an impact on the planning and ultimate lack of execution for Operation Hercules.

Results and Lessons Learned

Results

While many German leaders looked at the capture of Crete as a strategic victory there were also those who saw it as a hollow one. In relation to the other campaigns to this point in the war, the casualties on Crete were very high. The Germans suffered over 6,500 casualties out of 22,000 men dropped on the island--14,000 of these were parachute troops and the rest belonged to the mountain division. Much of the loss was due to bad landings because there were very few suitable spots in Crete, and the prevailing winds blew from the interior towards the sea. This was a result of being unable to plan properly due to lack of time to conduct a proper reconnaissance that caused aircraft to come into the landing zones from the wrong direction.[42] There is much debate about the specifics of the German losses on Crete. The German after action reports give total losses varying between 3,986 and 6,453 men; however, Winston Churchill states that more than 4,000 graves were counted in the area of Maleme and Suda Bay and another thousand at Retimo and Heraklion. Along with the great losses in personnel the loss of transport aircraft was important too.[43] Almost a third of the Ju-52s, 170 planes, used in the operation were damaged or destroyed.[44]

Germany was not the only country to suffer heavy losses. The British and Commonwealth forces suffered almost 3,500 casualties of which just over 1,700 were killed and almost 12,000 were taken prisoner, including Lieutenant Colonel Walker's entire 2/7 Australian Battalion, while the Greeks had approximately 10,000 men taken prisoner. Still, just as at Dunkirk and again in Greece, the Royal Navy evacuated almost 18,000 British soldiers from Sphakia. The Royal Navy lost three cruisers and six destroyers sunk; and one aircraft carrier, two battleships, six cruisers and seven destroyers were badly damaged, with the loss of over 2,000 men. The RAF lost some forty-seven aircraft in the battle. It is still unknown exactly how many Greek soldiers and Cretan civilians died during the fighting.[45]

In the wake of the final Allied evacuation of Crete on 1 June and the subsequent surrender of the remaining Allied forces, the occupied island was divided into two zones. The main German zone covered the western provinces of Hania, Retimo and Heraklion, while the subsidiary Italian zone covered the provinces of Sitia and Lasithi to the east.[46] At the conclusion of the successful Balkan campaign, General Geisler argued that the natural German supply route to North Africa now was by way of Greece and Crete instead of through Italy and by the British held island of Malta.[47]

In the end, the possession of Crete proved of little offensive value to the Axis Powers due to subsequent developments in the overall situation that prevented them from exploiting their success. The Russian campaign, which started twenty-one days after cessation of hostilities in Crete, led to a withdrawal of German air power from the eastern Mediterranean. To the Germans, Crete was not a stepping-stone to the Suez and the Middle East, but rather the concluding phase of the campaign in the Balkans.[48]

Lessons Learned

The invasion of Crete was a special operation and a number of lessons with general validity for similar operations were learned from the German experience.[49] An equal number were drawn from the common experiences of the combatants on Crete. The most significant was the importance of air power in providing support to the ground troops and its impact on naval operations. The German leadership and initiative, especially at the tactical level, also contributed to the outcome. The German airborne forces were relatively well equipped but their operational planning was flawed due to poor intelligence. The lack of surprise resulted in high casualties and brought the operations perilously close to failure. Had it not been for the support of Von Richthofen's Fliegerkorps VIII and the leadership and initiative qualities shown by the German officers, particularly the junior commanders, the battle would have been lost.

The numerically superior but poorly equipped Allied garrison came very close to winning the battle, but the key commanders failed to understand both the threat from and the vulnerabilities of an airborne force. Thus they were unable to grasp the necessary opportunities to win. They also missed the opportunity to launch an aggressive counterattack at the decisive point of the battle.

The role of the Luftwaffe using its immense advantage in combat power helped restrict the impact made by the Royal Navy. Air power was also able to support the beleaguered paratroopers, demoralize the defenders and interdict allied troop movements through out the battle. The casualty figures on both sides show higher than usual killed-to-wounded rates. This is a testament to the ferocity of the battle and how close the result was.[50]

Through careful analysis General Kurt Student and the other senior German airborne leaders drew specific lessons learned that were incorporated for future German airborne operations. They came away believing that the success of an airborne operation against an island would depend on the following factors:

a. Control of the air above the island is essential for the successful execution of airborne landings.
b. Control of the sea around the island is next in importance.
c. The command channels regulating inter-service cooperation must be clearly defined and unity of command over both airborne and seaborne forces must be firmly established
d. The element of surprise is essential to the success of an airborne operation that involves great risk under any circumstances.
e. Other important factors are the intensive collection of intelligence and proper and timely dissemination of information obtained.
f. Airborne tactics must be flexible.
g. Strong reserves, including flying formations, must be readily available so that any initial success, achieved wherever airborne landings have taken place, can be immediately exploited. Or, if unexpected difficulties arise. . . . These reserves must be capable of immediate effective counteraction.
h. Individual soldiers must carry light machine guns, recoilless rifles, rocket launchers, etc. during the descent in case they are forced to fight before recovering their parachutes.
i. The troops must be issued appropriate uniforms.[51]

Within twelve months the German airborne leaders would be planning the invasion of Malta. As will be shown in the discussion of Operation Hercules, all of these lessons were incorporated in the planning and training for the seizure of Malta.

Conclusion

Because of its daring execution and novel techniques employed, the airborne invasion of Crete was considered a historic military achievement. However, its many deficiencies, most of which were attributed to insufficient preparations, gave the operation all the characteristics of an improvisation. The capture of Crete was to provide a platform for the strategic purposes of protecting the Ploesti oilfields from British bombers and allowing German bombers access to bomb Alexandria and Cairo. These purposes were not met due to the withdrawal of the majority of Luftwaffe assets for the invasion of Russia less then on month later.[52]

Since military operations are not conducted in a vacuum and the enemy will also draw lessons learned, Operation Mercury had a dramatic affect on future airborne operations for both the Allies and the Axis. The Allies saw Crete as an operation displaying possibilities for their own future operations, and therefore encouraging the formation of large American and British airborne forces. However, the result was the exact opposite for Germany. Despite the success achieved, the high cost of the seizure of Crete led Hitler to lose confidence in airborne operations.[53] He was very upset by the heavy losses suffered by the parachute units on Crete, and came to the conclusion that the surprise value offered by airborne operations had passed.[54] Therefore as a result of the huge losses, the Fallschirmjaeger was forbidden to mount large-scale operations in the future. Apart from a few small-scale operations, the paratroopers mainly served as elite infantry for the rest of the war. In 1952 General Student stated that Crete was rightly dubbed the 'Graveyard of the Fallschirmjäger'.[55]

---

[1] Bruce Quarrie, *German Airborne Divisions: Mediterranean Theatre, 1942-1945* (Oxford, England: Osprey Publishing, 2005), 4.

[2] Maria Biank, *The Battle Of Crete: Hitler's Airborne Gamble* (Fort Leavenworth, Kansas: 2003), 20.

[3] Department of the Army, Department of the Army Pamphlet 20-260, *The German Campaigns in the Balkans (Spring 1941)* (Historical study, Department of the Army, November 1953), 121-123. (hereafter cited: DA PAM 20-260).

[4] Ibid., 119.

[5] Biank, 42.

[6] DA PAM 20-260, 119-123.

[7] Warlimont, 130.

[8] Lutton, 94-95.

[9] Biank, 1.

[10] DA PAM 20-260, 119-120.

[11] James Lucas, *Storming Eagles: German Airborne Forces in World War II* (Edison, New Jersey: Castle Books, 2004), 134.

[12] DA PAM 20-260, 120.

[13] Lutton, 95-96.

[14] Biank, 23.

[15] DA PAM 20-260, 120.

[16] Lutton, 96.

[17] Ibid., 96.

[18] DA PAM 20-260, 120.

[19] Peter Antill, *Crete 1941: Germany's Lightning Airborne Assault* (Oxford, England: Osprey Publishing, 2005), 32.

[20] DA PAM 20-260, 124.

[21] Antill, 32-33.

[22] Ibid., 33-34.

[23] Ibid., 33.

[24] DA PAM 20-260, 120-121.

[25] Antill, 34-36.

[26] DA PAM 20-260, 129.

[27] Ibid., 120.

[28] Ibid., 127-129.

[29] Lucas, 71.

[30] Ibid., 77-78.

[31] DA PAM 20-260, 127.

[32] Biank, 42

[33] DA PAM 20-260, 124.

[34] Biank, 42-43

[35] Antill, 34.

[36] DA PAM 20-260, 123.

[37] Antill, 34-35.

[38] DA PAM 20-260, 123.

[39] Antill, 35.

[40] DA PAM 20-260, 21-124.

[41] Antill, 36.

[42] Liddell Hart, B.H., *The German Generals Talk* (New York: Perennial, 1975), 160.

[43] DA PAM 20-260, 139.

[44] Antill, 87.

[45] Ibid., 87.

[46] Ibid., 88.

[47] Lutton, p.99.

[48] DA PAM 20-260, 147.

[49] Ibid., 141.

[50] Antill, 87.

[51] DA PAM 20-260, 141-147.

[52] Ibid., 147.

[53] Ibid., 147.

[54] Liddell Hart, *The German Generals Talk*, 160.

[55] Antill, 87.

CHAPTER 4

ATTACKING AND DEFENDING MALTA

1940

Shortly before 0700 on 11 June 1940, 10 Savoia-Marcherri 79 three-engine bombers took off from their base at Catania in Sicily to attack Malta for the very first time and began an expenditure in resources for the Axis that should have resulted in the defeat of a British outpost and permitted the conquest of the Mediterranean by Mussolini's new Roman Empire. However, this did not occur. In reality, Malta became a thorn in the plans of both Mussolini and Hitler up until the defeat of Italian and German forces in North Africa and the invasion of Sicily in July 1943 by the Allies.[1]

The declaration of war by Mussolini was against both France and Great Britain. The primary purpose that he gave for declaring war was "because the honor and interest of Italy requires it of us."[2] However, the reason was more selfish then the honor of Italy. Mussolini wanted a seat at the peace table when the German campaign in France ended. Italy's problem was that instead of declaring war against an impoverished third world country like Abyssinia, Ethiopia, or Albania, this time it was against two of its former World War I Allies. Both of these countries were more then capable of holding their own against Italy even when near defeat against Germany, as France was. When Italy invaded France only days before France surrendered to Germany, the Italian Army was thrown back into its own territory.

When Italy began attacking Malta, it did so only from the air. At no point did Italy try to seize Malta from the British. This situation surprised many people on both sides. Britain, although relieved that an assault of the island did not occur, was surprised because it felt that even the Italians could have easily captured the island. Even Mussolini's ally, Hitler, was astonished at the failure of Italy to seize Malta at the outset of hostilities because he understood how important it was for Italy to maintain open lines of communications with its troops in North Africa.[3] The seizure of Malta from the outset would have accomplished this. Italy's failure at this point would come back to haunt both Italy and Germany for the remainder of the war in the Mediterranean and could be considered to be a fundamental strategic blunder.[4] This decision also had the effect of eroding the relationship between Germany and Italy.[5] Hitler would hold this operational failure against Mussolini and the Italian armed forces for the remainder of the war, and in 1942 used it as an excuse not to conduct an operation against Malta.

After the first air attack on 11 June 1940, thirty-five bombers escorted by eighteen fighters conducted a high level attack against the naval base at La Valetta, the air base at Hal Far, and the flying boat base at Kalafrana. That afternoon they executed another raid with five bombers against La Valetta and thirty-three bombers escorted by twelve fighters against Hal Far and Kalafrana. When the Italians returned for their afternoon raid they were met by the first air defense of Malta. Two Gloster biplanes sortied to intercept the Italian attack, but did not shoot down any Italian aircraft.[6] As the attacks continued over the next few days more and more families that lived around the harbor area were forced to seek shelter in the towns and village further inland. The raids would become part of the pattern of daily life for the Maltese civilians, but the Italians would not sustain the intensity of the initial raids.[7] As the British began to reinforce the island's defenses the raids continued to diminish in both intensity and effect. In August Malta was bombed on only five days. In September that number was only four, and these were conducted by small formations of bombers escorted by Fiat biplanes and Macci 200s and caused only minimal damage. The effects and intensity of the Italian raids even became a joke among the other branches of the Italian military. The official Air Force communiqués would constantly report that Malta had "been bombed again with considerable results." The joke that ended up being circulated around the Navy showed the failure of the Italian propaganda: "a news announcement, so ran the jest, would read that the Germans had entered London and hoisted the swastika over Buckingham Palace, the Japanese had captured Washington, and the Italians had again 'bombed Malta with considerable results.'"[8] Asides from being a joke, this was also far from the actual effects of the bombing. The Italian bombing did very little damage when they actually delivered their bombs near the target, and when they encountered Malta's fighter or antiaircraft defenses the Italian bombers often dropped their bombs in the sea and returned to base.[9] This remained the case throughout 1940, especially after the British started reinforcing the island with aircraft and antiaircraft artillery.

Once the British figured out that the Italians were not going to assault the island they began to reinforce it and make it into both a defensive fortress in the middle of the Mediterranean and an offensive platform to attack first Italian and later German assets. The British had started fortifying the island prior to declaring war on Germany in September 1939, but since there was no war against Italy the pace of building up the defenses was slow and considered a low priority by the leaders in London. In September 1939 the garrison consisted of 4,000 troops that included four British infantry battalions.[10] In October 1939 work was started on three tarmac strips at the new aerodrome of Luqa. It was completed two months before Italy declared war. Once Italy entered the war obstructions were placed at the ends of the three runways to prevent enemy aircraft from landing. On 28 June 1940 Luqa became operational. This was necessary to support the air defense of Malta that would prove invaluable.[11]

Prior to June 1940 it was estimated that at least four squadrons of fighters would be necessary to defend Malta, but it was clear to the military leadership on Malta that there was little to no chance of receiving these aircraft because the defense of the British Isles was the top priority. Initially the only aircraft on the island were a few obsolete London II flying boats, whose pilots had no knowledge of flying in a fighter aircraft. However, an unexpected cache of unassembled Gloster Gladiators was found. This came as a pleasant surprise and the aircraft were quickly assembled. Once the planes were assembled the problem of qualified pilots arose. Although there were no trained pilots many people volunteered and by the time of the first Italian raids a flight of seven pilots was assembled.[12]

When the Italians started bombing Malta the British defenders were able to use these few outdated aircraft to defend the island. The Bristol Gloster Gladiators were outdated all-metal biplanes that had a top speed of 257 mph and were armed with four .30 caliber machine guns and were no longer in front line service in the Royal Air Force. During the first several weeks of the war in the Mediterranean these few planes were the only air opposition to the Regia Aeronautica in the skies over Malta. As part of a British information operation it was claimed at the time that there were only three planes flying against the Italians. These three planes were christened <u>Hope</u>, <u>Faith</u>, and <u>Charity</u>. Although there were more then just three planes defending there were not the twenty-five fighters defending the island as the Italian Air Staff reported. This was an exaggeration but it lent credibility to how determined the British were to defend the island, which helped British morale. It also showed the Italians that the island would be defended at any cost.[13]

As the Italian raids started, the air defense of Malta was not the only area in need of fixing. Almost every other area was suffering from critical shortages as well. The original defense plan for Malta was designed to protect against a likely surprise seaborne invasion, so much was done to concentrate on the coastal defenses, especially around Grand Harbor near La Valetta on the Northeastern coast, the eastern coast, and Marsaxlokk (Marsa Scirocco) Bay on the southeastern corner of the island. The rest of the island was considered secure from any seaborne invasion because of the cliffs.[14] However, once it was realized that the Italians would not invade the island but instead bomb it the focus became the air and anti-aircraft defenses. In early June 1940 the British Chiefs of Staff analyzed the defense preparations for Malta and decided that 'there is nothing practicable we can do to increase the powers of resistance of Malta." This changed by the end of the summer with the increase in aircraft to the island and by the end of the year the island was not only able to defend itself, but also to conduct offensive operations against the Italians.[15]

The initial aircraft situation on the island was dismal; however, the status of the anti-aircraft (AA) defenses was no better. The British had decided to build up the Malta anti-aircraft defenses to a level of 122 heavy AA guns, 60 light AA guns, and 24 searchlights. However, by June 1940 the searchlights were the only part of the system that was close to the needed number. There were only 34 heavy AA guns and eight light

AA guns on the island and not all of them were operational when the first air raids occurred.[16]

Just as in Great Britain steps were taken to create a force from the local population to assist with a possible invasion. On 3 June 1940 the Malta Volunteer Defense Force was created. It was formed primarily from the local hunters and farmers with the main task of shooting at any airborne invasion force. It later was renamed the Malta Home Guard, and was organized similarly to the British Home Guard. As with the British Home Guard it increased in strength and experience as time went on.[17]

Although building the anti-aircraft defenses and establishing a Home Guard were important, the single most important defensive requirement was fighter aircraft and the pilots to fly them. Because the initial air defense proved that the island could be defended, British leaders decided that Malta should be equipped with the necessary aircraft. Admiral Cunningham, the Commander-in-Chief for the Mediterranean Theater, sent a request to the First Sea Lord of the Admiralty, Admiral Sir Dudley Pound, on 27 June 1940 for fighter aircraft reinforcements. Within that request he laid down what was needed for Malta:

> I suppose the broad Naval Strategy will require some reconsidering. I hope it will not be necessary to abandon the Eastern Mediterranean: the landslide would be frightful. . . . Malta is doing very well, I think, and the morale of the Maltese is surprisingly high. . . . Six days ago they were down to the last one of the Gladiator Fleet Air Arm spare aircraft I told them to use. Is it even now too late to get the Air Ministry to send out some fighters? If we had twenty or thirty fighters at Malta ready to operate over the fleet I think we could guarantee to make the Sicilians, anyway, very sorry that Italy entered the war. I am sure that the provision of aircraft for Malta would make all the difference to our operations both in the Eastern and Western Mediterranean.[18]

By the end of the month four Hawker Hurricanes that had been scheduled for the defense of the Royal Navy base at Alexandria were diverted to Malta.[19]

Within two weeks of Admiral Cunningham's request to the First Sea Lord, Prime Minister Churchill directed that Admiral Pound increase the defenses of Malta. Part of that directive read: "'2: It becomes of high and immediate importance to build up a very strong anti-aircraft defense at Malta, and to base several squadrons of our best fighter aircraft there."[20] At the time this was a very difficult decision to make. Aircraft and ammunition were in short supply after the surrender of France and only a few weeks prior to the Battle of Britain. This decision was a strong indicator of how important Churchill felt that Malta was both strategically and as a source to boost British morale. Churchill understood the situation in Britain and knew that as well as controlling the central Mediterranean the success of defending Malta would help increase British morale after the desperate evacuation of the British and Allied forces at Dunkirk.

Churchill wanted to first hold Malta, and then when the level of supplies permitted to use it as an offensive platform for attacks against Axis forces in the Mediterranean. Even though fighter aircraft were in short supply everywhere, Malta received twelve Hurricanes in August. The aircraft resupply was continued until the siege of the island ended in 1943. The resupply was primarily conducted using aircraft carriers to ferry the aircraft within the flying range of Malta and then the aircraft would take off and fly to Malta while the aircraft carrier remained safely out of range of enemy air and sea assets in either Europe or Africa.[21]

Along with the increase in fighter aircraft on Malta, the British War Cabinet felt it important to base surface warships at Malta in order to conduct offensive operations against Italy. Prior to Italy declaring war Admiral Cunningham made the decision to move the British fleet stationed at Malta to Alexandria because of the potential threat of

Italian air and sea attacks against Malta, and of the feeling that Malta would be lost shortly after hostilities commenced. In fact, when Italy entered the war the Royal Navy had only six submarines at Malta. All other ships conducted operations from either Alexandria or Gibraltar.[22] Once the decision was made to defend Malta the War Cabinet urged Admiral Cunningham to base surface ships at Malta. This moving of ships was not immediate, but by October 1940 the Admiralty released four ships from the Home Fleet to be stationed at Malta. From this point Malta was able to take an offensive posture not only from the air, but also at sea.[23]

The effect on the Italians was immediate. The Italian Navy already feared an engagement with the Royal Navy coming from Gibraltar or Alexandria. But when ships were returned to Malta the Italian Navy believed it would suffer a terrible defeat at the hands of the British in Italian home waters. Then the Royal Navy would be able to 'ramble about the Mediterranean inflicting whatever damage it wants to our scarcely defended coast.' The Italians were not the only ones to feel that this was the case. The German leadership, specifically Adolf Hitler, believed that the Italians would run from any engagement against the British.[24]

By the end of 1940 the effect that the Italians had on Malta was almost nothing. It was only during the first few weeks of the war that the air raids were constant, and sometimes up to six raids a day were conducted.[25] However, by August and into September, the Italian bombing raids were intermittent and had little effect on the island infrastructure or the morale of the defenders and its citizens. The Italian Navy was unable to isolate the island and prevent the British from repositioning warships at Malta. On the other hand, the effects that the British in Malta had on the Italian war in the

Mediterranean were quite significant. Along with air raids against Malta, Italian forces were conducting an offensive campaign in North Africa. One of the requirements for this offensive was to resupply the army from Italy. This required convoys from ports in Italy to travel to the ports of Tripoli and Benghazi in Libya. The convoys were within range of the fighters on Malta.[26] Part of the reason for the air raids against Malta was to permit the unmolested movement of the supply convoys. But because of the failed attempts to bomb Malta, the British fighters were not only able to defeat the Italian bombers, but were also able to focus on attacking Italian convoys for the remainder of 1940. These attacks had some effect on the Italian invasion of British Somaliland in August 1940, but would have a definite impact on the Italian invasion of Egypt in September 1940. Although the Italians were able to invade Egypt, they were unable to push farther then Sidi Barrani, 65 miles inside Egypt's border with Libya.[27] Then in November when the Italians invaded Greece and became bogged down there, the aircraft from Malta were able to take offensive action against targets in Sicily and Italy.

Germany began to show an interest in the Mediterranean and North Africa as early as August 1940. At the time, Hitler refused to take an active role in the theater but did offer to loan Mussolini German armored units for the fight in North Africa. In September the German naval liaison officer in Rome, Vice Admiral Eberhard Weichold, attempted to generate German interest in an attack on Malta. He put together a detailed report in August calling for the elimination of Malta. He followed that report up with another in September that recommended that German aircraft, submarines and light surface units be sent to the Mediterranean. Speaking about the elimination of Malta he stated:

> Malta is the stumbling block of Italy's conduct of the war at[sic] sea. . . . If the Italian navy is to fulfill its main function, which is to keep open sea communications with Libya, then --from the purely military standpoint--it must take action immediately and forestall the British by eliminating Malta and capturing Crete. Both of [sic] these operations, if carefully prepared and launched without warning, have excellent prospect of success, though the latter would certainly entail a degree of risk.[28]

Germany was forced to take an active interest in the war in the Mediterranean Theater when Italy invaded Greece on 28 October 1940. Within two weeks the Greeks stopped the Italian offensive and by the end of November the Italians were pushed back into Albania. For a second time in 1940 Italy had conducted a military blunder that would affect the relationship with Germany and change the conduct of the war in the Mediterranean. Mussolini never told Hitler of his plans to invade Greece. When Hitler found out about the pending invasion he arranged to meet with Mussolini in Florence to urge Mussolini not to attack. However, by the time they met at the station in Florence Mussolini informed Hitler that Italian troops were on the march into Greece.[29] Because of Hitler's plans to invade the Soviet Union in 1941 Germany needed a secure flank in the Balkans and the use of bases in Romania as a staging area for the invasion. This situation was upset by the Italian invasion of Greece. Shortly after the Italian invasion began General Wavell, the British commander in Egypt, was ordered to send 30,000 troops from North Africa to Greece to support the Greeks. At this point Hitler felt it necessary to invade Greece in order to secure Germany's right flank in the Balkans.

1941

The German invasion of the Balkans saved the Italians, who were still on the defensive against the Greeks. While preparing to invade the Balkans Hitler also felt it necessary to support the Italians in North Africa. In February 1941 the Afrika Korps under the command of Generalleutnant Erwin Rommel was sent to Libya to prop up the failed Italian operations against the British. Rommel's forces arrived in Tripoli and were ordered to take a defensive posture; however, Rommel decided to go on the offensive and bring the Mediterranean Theater and North Africa into the forefront for the next two years.

From the beginning of the German intervention in the Mediterranean its strategy was flawed. Unlike Churchill, who understood from the outset of the war that Malta was a strategic link in Britain's supply line to the Middle East and the Pacific, Hitler always saw Malta and the Mediterranean as a sideshow to what he was doing on the continent of Europe. He was never fully convinced of Malta's strategic impact, although when the supply situation in North Africa became an issue, he did feel it necessary to attack Malta in order to allow the flow of supplies to the Afrika Korps.[30]

Just like Italy, when Germany began operations in the Mediterranean, it never attempted to seize Malta; in fact, it did not even give priority to attacking the airfields and the defenses of Malta. The priority was given to supporting Rommel's troops in North Africa and to reducing the supplies coming to North Africa for the Allied armies. The first Luftwaffe raid against Malta in early 1941 was a case in point. It was a raid of opportunity, not to destroy aircraft or to damage shipping or harbor infrastructure. Instead it was to attack the British aircraft carrier HMS *Illustrious*, which was ferrying aircraft to resupply Malta. *Illustrious* was considered the pride of the Royal Navy because of its ability to sustain damage and survive. The Germans believed that if the *Illustrious* were sunk it would be a crippling blow to British morale. So, when *Illustrious* came into the Mediterranean with a supply of aircraft for Malta the Germans were ready to destroy her.

German bombers intercepted the aircraft carrier a hundred miles west of Malta, but were unable to sink her. They did score several direct hits, but the carrier was able to repel the German bombers and reach Grand Harbor with its cargo intact. The Germans continued to attack, not the harbor, but focused on this single ship in an attempt to sink it. During the first German air raid after the ship arrived in harbor it sustained only one direct hit, on the quarterdeck. The *Illustrious* remained in harbor for most of January 1941 and endured many more attacks by the Luftwaffe, but was able to depart Malta on 23 January 1941. The Germans expended significant assets against a single target and were unable to sink it, nor even cause any major damage to it.[31]

Along with attempting to cripple British morale by attacking HMS *Illustrious* the Luftwaffe began to assist the Italian Air Force with raids against the island itself. These raids were haphazard and did little damage and were very similar to the Italian raids of late summer 1940. Not until February 1941 did the German air attacks on Malta become significant. Mussolini and Hitler finally came to an agreement and the Luftwaffe was instructed to aid the Italians in capturing the island. No attempts were actually made to capture the island in 1941, but Hitler also used this cooperation as a way to secure the sea-lanes for the supply convoys that ran from southern Italy to North Africa. In February the raids increased and by the end of the month the fighter attacks against Malta caused significant losses including the deaths of all the British flight commanders. By March most of the air defenses on Malta were either destroyed or damaged so badly that they were no longer serviceable.[32]

Even during the German invasion of the Balkans begun in April 1941 the bombing of the island continued. The British were able to reinforce the island with aircraft and pilots in April and again in May. Despite the continued bombing the defenders were able to protect the island well enough to allow resupply convoys to reach the island.[33] However, because of plans for Operation Barbarossa the Luftwaffe assets dedicated to attacking Malta were shifted to the east for that pending invasion. This reduced the raids against Malta to the occasional Italian raid for the remainder of 1941.

For a period in the spring of 1941 there was a possibility of a German invasion of Malta. Großadmiral Erich Raeder, Commander-in-Chief of the German Navy, recommended occupying Malta in order to protect convoys going to North Africa. However, Hitler showed little interest in such an endeavor after hearing from the Luftwaffe about how difficult it would be to attack Malta because of the stonewalls that were located throughout the island. These walls were designed to separate personal property and would cause severe damage to paratroopers as they landed.[34] Instead, Hitler chose Crete because of its larger airfields, good anchorage, and the need to protect the Romanian oilfields from British bombers attacking it from Crete and Egypt. So, by the end of May 1941, Germany invaded Crete and forced the British and Commonwealth troops to evacuate to Egypt.

Germany's operations against Malta from February to April gave validity to the need to secure the island. During the German and Italian raids from February into April, only one Axis ship that transited the routes from Italy to North Africa was lost from British air interdiction from Malta. This proved that when pressure was applied against Malta, it was possible to move convoys across the Mediterranean. The question was whether the intensity of the raids could be sustained?

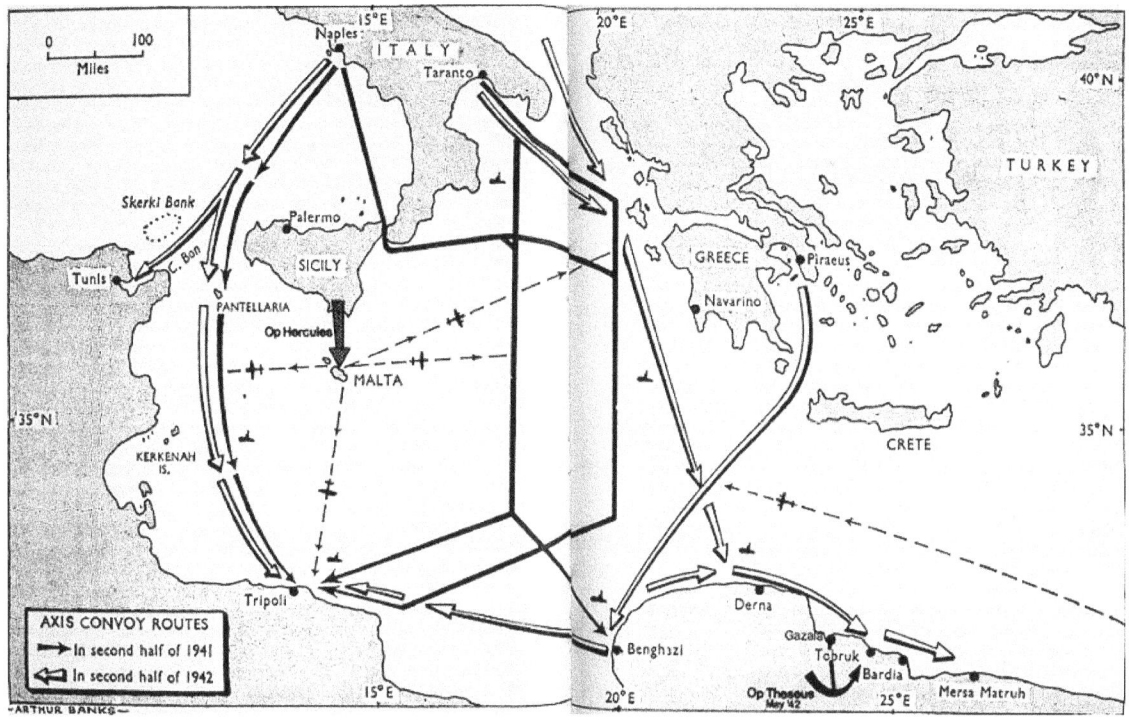

Figure 3. Axis convoy routes 1941-1942
Source: Kenneth Macksey, *Kesselring, German Master Strategist of the Second World War* (London, England: Greenhill Books, 1996), 108-109.

This question was answered with the end of the Balkan campaign. Requirements for the upcoming invasion of the Soviet Union necessitated the transfer of X Fliegerkorps from Sicily and the Germans returned the main effort for bombing Malta to the Italians.[35] The German planes that remained in the Mediterranean Theater were busy supporting Rommel's operations in North Africa. The Italian raids for the remainder of the summer and fall of 1941, about 60 or 70 sorties a week, were no more effective or intensive then the raids of late 1940. Because of the Italians' failure to maintain pressure on Malta, the British were given a reprieve to rebuild their defenses and resupply their fighter aircraft. Throughout the summer of 1941 the British were able to ferry fighters to the island fortress from the aircraft carriers HMS *Victorious*, HMS *Ark Royal*, and HMS *Furious*. In

June 1941, 139 Hurricane fighters arrived on the island. These aircraft were not only successful in protecting the island but also presented a constant threat to Rommel's supply line between Europe and North Africa.[36]

Although the Germans were not conducting raids on Malta, they were still suffering from the losses due to Malta's offensive operations. The German liaison staff working with the Italian Air Force reported on the activity in the Central Mediterranean during the period from 11 July to 31 August 1941. The main element of this report was that the most dangerous weapon the British had were their submarines operating from Malta. The report estimated that during the period covered there were 36 submarine attacks that resulted in at least 19 ships sunk, eight of those ships being sunk within sight of Tripoli or Benghazi. Malta's sea and air forces continued to attack Axis shipping with considerable results.[37] Count Ciano recorded in his diary at the end of September that the situation in the Mediterranean was serious because of the continued loss of merchant shipping. Less then two weeks later, he wrote again that the supply situation in Libya was becoming "more and more difficult" because only twenty percent of the supplies scheduled for North Africa actually made it to Libya. The situation became so grave that in mid October the Italian Navy started sending troops and supplies across in warships.[38] These were sometimes referred to as "battleship convoys" crossing the Mediterranean mostly at night and at high speed. This became the new standing procedure for transporting troops, which only increased the problem of supplying them.(see figure 3)

The supply situation in the Mediterranean and North Africa in November 1941 was considered by Hitler to be desperate. This caused him to move one of his most able air commanders on the Russian front, Feldmarschall Albert Kesselring and his staff of the

II Luftflotte, from the central sector facing Moscow to the Mediterranean front. Kesselring, who was fluent in Italian, was selected because of his ability to be diplomatic with his Italian counter part, Count Cavallero, the Chief of the Italian Commando Supremo. Although Kesselring was designated Commander-in-Chief South, he was not given the authority to exercise direct command over all German and Italian forces in the Mediterranean, but had to go through Commando Supremo, even with Rommel's Afrika Korps.[39]

The II Fliegerkorps was also pulled from the Russian Front, and after being reequipped was sent back to Sicily in December 1941. With other reinforcements sent to the Mediterranean front, Hitler issued Kesselring War directive 38, on December 2, 1941, which assigned three broad missions.

> 1. To secure mastery of the air and sea in the area between southern Italy and North Africa in order to secure communications with Libya and Cyrenaica and, in particular, to keep Malta in subjection.
> 2. To co-operate with German and allied forces engaged in North Africa.
> 3. To paralyze enemy traffic through the Mediterranean and British supplies to Tobruk and Malta, in close cooperation with the German and Italian naval forces available for this task.[40]

Until the II Fliegerkorps transferred to the Mediterranean, no more then 70 Axis aircraft were operating against Malta. As 1941 closed that number of attacking aircraft was tripled and the amount of bombs dropped on Malta increased by 10 times. During December 1941, the scene changed dramatically in the Mediterranean. At the beginning of the month the Italians were on the verge of abandoning their resupply efforts to North Africa, but by the end of the month, the Luftwaffe was back in force and reestablishing its aerial siege of Malta. On 22 December 1941, Kesselring initiated an air offensive against Malta. This drastically altered the previous pattern of attacks. This new offensive saw raids with over 200 aircraft taking part. With the loss in fighting the Japanese in the Pacific it looked as if the British might be on the verge of losing two major areas, North Africa and Malaya.[41]

Resupplying Malta

Before considering the operations against Malta in 1942 it is important to discuss the resupplying of Malta. Until the Italians and Germans were defeated in North Africa, one of the main tasks of the British sea and air forces on Malta was to interdict and destroy the Axis convoys that were sending supplies to North Africa. The British used all the resources possible to accomplish this task. Just like the British, the Germans and Italians did everything possible to stop the convoys that were attempting to resupply Malta. From the summer of 1940 through December 1942, the British sent ten large and fourteen smaller convoys from either Gibraltar or Alexandria. In all; twenty-four separate convoys, plus seven individual ships and numerous different resupply operations by submarines and other warships made the passage to Malta. These convoys brought in food, munitions, especially anti-aircraft ammunition, and all the other necessities the soldiers and civilians needed to survive.[42]

On more than one occasion, these convoys saved Malta from the brink of disaster and altered the fighting for Malta. As soon as the decision was made to make Malta a fortress in the central Mediterranean the British arranged to send a convoy to Malta. This convoy arrived in August 1940 and brought in 40,000 tons of supplies. Again in the summer of 1941 after the Luftwaffe had pounded the island through February and March, and after the battle of Crete was over, a convoy of eleven merchant ships with three escorts brought in 65,000 tons of supplies.[43] Again in September, eight merchant ships brought in 85,000 tons of supplies.[44] This convoy was the last for 1941. To supply Malta the British lost only one merchant ship out of thirty-nine that sailed. The Royal Navy had one cruiser and one destroyer sunk, and one battleship, two cruisers, and one destroyer damaged while escorting the convoys.[45] The most perilous times for resupplying Malta were to come in 1942.

Along with the convoys that brought the needed supplies to Malta there were twenty seven resupply operations to replenish the aircraft defending Malta. A total of 766 aircraft were ferried, of which 720 arrived safely on the island. The primary means of ferrying aircraft to Malta were by aircraft carriers. Through 1940 and 1941, the aircraft carriers HMS *Argus, Ark Royal, Furious,* and *Eagle* were used. Once the United States entered the war the American aircraft carrier USS *Wasp* was employed to ferry aircraft. These operations originated primarily from Gibraltar. When they were within flying range the aircraft would fly the remainder of the distance. As the statistics show, this was an effective method of getting aircraft to Malta. Of the forty-six aircraft that did not make it to Malta only thirty-four were permanently lost.[46]

In the summer of 1940, sending planes to Malta was a controversial issue, especially since it came shortly after the end of the Battle of France and while the British leadership was planning for what became the Battle of Britain. The first aircraft were Hawker Hurricanes that arrived at the end of June 1940 and remained the primary fighter defense for Malta until March 1942 when the first fifteen Spitfires flew from the HMS *Eagle* and *Argus*. This was the first deployment of Spitfires outside the British Isles.

Although the majority of the aircraft made it to the island safely, it does not mean that they arrived unobserved. On several occasions German aircraft arrived to bomb the airfields and newly arrived aircraft.

Strategic Update

Before analyzing the operations against Malta it is necessary to provide an update on the strategic situation up to September 1942. The biggest change of the war in 1942 was the introduction of the United States as an active participant following the Japanese attack on Pearl Harbor and the German declaration of war against the Americans. Although it would take most of the year before the U.S. was able to mount a ground operation into North Africa, the impact of the industrial base and the active U.S. contribution in fighting the Battle of the Atlantic greatly assisted Great Britain and increased the use of war materiel by Britain in their campaigns in 1942.

When the Japanese attacked the U.S. Fleet at Pearl Harbor, they also began attacking American, Dutch, and British possessions in the Far East. Great Britain had to deal with this threat to its Asian empire. This came from the Japanese invasion of Malaya on 8 December 1941. The landings were unopposed and the Japanese, although outnumbered, moved with little hindrance towards Singapore. General Arthur Percival surrendered Singapore on 17 February 1942, and 130,000 British and Commonwealth troops marched into captivity. On 10 December 1941, the Japanese sank the HMS *Prince of Wales* and HMS *Repulse*. These ships were part of a fleet sent to shore up the defenses of Singapore. The fleet was sent without any air cover, and was attacked by land based torpedo bombers. The battleship HMS *Prince of Wales* was the pride of the Royal Navy and was sunk with the loss of 840 sailors and marines.[47] Again this proved the importance of land based aircraft on naval operations.

While the Malaya campaign was underway the Japanese invaded Burma and began marching towards Rangoon. Japanese troops invaded through Siam, present day Thailand, on 16 January 1942. By March 8th Japanese forces entered Rangoon. The British finally decided to abandon Burma on 25 April. The Japanese control of Burma would direct British strategy in Southeast Asia until 1944.[48]

The third main setback for the British in the Far East came in the form of raids against Ceylon, present day Sri Lanka, by the First Air Fleet. The intent of the raids was to attack allied installations at on Ceylon. The raids were conducted from 5-9 April and were successful. The First Air Fleet managed to wipe out the British aircraft on the ground and sink the aircraft carrier HMS *Hermes* and other capital ships in its attacks. Although the raids were a significant blow to British prestige, it had no long lasting strategic significance for the Japanese. In fact Admiral Nagumo, the Commander of the First Air Fleet, stated that the raids were a waste of time, resources, and such a highly trained force.[49]

Although in 1941 the Battle of the Atlantic appeared to be going against the German U-boats, they reemerged with the entrance of the United States into the war. 1942 saw the largest amount of shipping losses by tonnage of the war. However, by the middle of the year it was evident that the U-boat force was beginning to lose the battle again. The majority of allied losses were coming from the Arctic convoys to the Soviet Union because of the integrated U-boat and air attack against those convoys. By the end of 1942, through the exploitation of Ultra, the British decoding of German Enigma traffic, and the lessons learned by both the British and American navies, the Allies were making it very dangerous for the U-boats everywhere.[50]

For the Italians, not much had changed in 1942. They were still fully committed in North Africa and providing an entire field army to the German forces on the Russian Front. Although the Italians were in overall command in the Mediterranean, it was more and more evident that without the support of German troops and materiel the Italians would have collapsed long before the beginning of 1942.

At the beginning of 1942, Germany's main focus was on the Russian front where their forces were in retreat from the battle of Moscow. This was the first retreat authorized for German forces in the war. Through the rest of the winter and into the early spring both German and Soviet forces were regrouping and preparing for summer operations. In the spring, Hitler and the OKW began planning for the 1942 offensive. The original plan was to continue the advance against Moscow with a smaller attack against Leningrad.[51] By April, Hitler, who had taken personal command of the Army Groups in the Soviet Union, changed the plan and only authorized the operations for Army Group South. This was a total change from what the OKW recommended, and showed the influence of Hitler's control in planning and conducting operations. The difference between this offensive and that of 1941 was that the goal was not the capture of Moscow or the destruction of the Soviet army in the field. Instead the goal was first the capture of the Crimea in the South and then to secure the resources, especially the oil rich areas of the Caucasus region. Although it was not planned, by the end of the year, Germany would be on the verge of suffering the greatest defeat of the war at Stalingrad.[52] It was this campaign that would have the biggest impact on the German operations in the Mediterranean and against Malta.

1942

With the attacks on Malta increasing, it appeared as if 1942 would be a good year for the Axis in the Mediterranean. The II Luftflotte had almost 400 out of 650 operational aircraft, two-thirds of its strength, to dedicate to conducting the offensive against Malta. Because of the success of attacks against Malta, the Italians decided to send two convoys to North Africa in January. Both convoys arrived without any losses. This influx of supplies enabled Rommel to launch a new offensive against the British on 21 January 1942. The day after Rommel started his offensive, the Italians sent another "battleship convoy" to North Africa.[53]

As the assault picked up against Malta Field Marshal Kesselring issued a set of instructions to the German and Italian Naval forces for operations against Malta at the end of January. These instructions included:

>   --On February 2, the blockade of the Sicilian Channel would begin;
>   --Axis submarines would operate between Crete and Cyrenaica to help block the way to the island;
>   --The approaches to Malta would be mined between February 10 and 20.[54]

In these new instructions, Kesselring was using all possible assets against Malta. To further increase pressure against Malta in February the II Luftflotte flew 2299 sorties against Malta while the Italians flew an additional 791. These new attacks did cause a decrease in the effectiveness of Malta's defenders but did not prevent a convoy from arriving at Malta with badly needed supplies.[55] In January 1942, one small convoy and two individual ships were sent to Malta. These were the last ships that made it to Malta with little opposition until November, after the Allied invasion of Northwest Africa. Even with the arrival of these convoys, the island faced starvation. It was necessary to send more supplies to Malta.[56]

In February, Admiral Cunningham decided to try to send another convoy to Malta. He knew it was a serious risk due to the increase in Axis pressure on the island. Even the British War Cabinet knew that if a convoy did not reach Malta, the food would only last until May. They also knew that because of Axis strength in the Western Mediterranean this convoy would have to come from Alexandria.[57]

The convoy sailed in March and had a dangerous journey that resulted in only a small portion of the needed supplies arriving safely. The convoy labeled MW 10 consisted of 4 merchant ships. It left Alexandria on 20 March and managed to avoid enemy contact until 22 March. That day a German transport aircraft flying from Libya to Crete spotted the convoy. An Italian Navy task force consisting of the battleship *Littorio*, two heavy cruisers, one light cruiser, and ten destroyers happened to be at sea. The British escorts of four light cruisers, one anti-aircraft cruiser, and thirteen destroyers were informed of this development and managed to keep the merchant ships away from the Italian warships.[58] The Italians did sink three destroyers, one submarine, and one merchant ship, and damaged one merchant ship, but more importantly they delayed the arrival of the convoy into Grand Harbor by several hours.[59] This meant that instead of arriving under the cover of darkness the two remaining ships made it into Grand Harbor on the morning of 23 March. The Luftwaffe attacked the ships shortly after they arrived and sank all three merchant ships in the Harbor. Of the 5,000 tons of supplies that arrived in Grand Harbor, only 1,000 tons were unloaded before the ships were sunk. Although the convoy and most of the supplies were destroyed, the failure of the Italian Navy to destroy the convoy at sea caused both the German and Italian air forces to lose confidence in the capabilities of the Italian Navy.[60] With the failure of convoy MW-10 the War Cabinet realized that they must push another convoy to Malta. They planned for two convoys to go to Malta one from each end of the Mediterranean, running simultaneously. However, these convoys were not scheduled until June 1942 leaving Malta to survive for at least two more months before being resupplied.[61]

With the destruction of the March convoy, the Luftwaffe returned to its plan of attack, and focused on attacking against the naval installations in and around Grand Harbor. The attacks were so severe that the submarine forces in the harbor were forced to remain submerged during the day to limit damage from the attacks and had to surface at night to make necessary repairs. In the process of the attacks, twenty-one ships were sunk in the harbor and its approaches and thirteen more were damaged. In April, the remaining surface and submarine forces were forced to withdraw from Malta for the safety of Gibraltar and Alexandria.[62]

Earlier in the month, the first Spitfires arrived in Malta. As mentioned before, this was the first time the Spitfires were deployed outside the British Isles. This decision was made not because they had the extra Spitfires to deploy to Malta but because of necessity. By early 1942, the British realized that the Hurricanes and the American built P-40 Kittyhawks, used by RAF squadrons in the Middle East, were outmatched in combat by the new German "F" model Me. 109s and Italian Macchi 202s. On 7 March, fifteen Spitfires along with four Blenheim light bombers were flown off the aircraft carriers

HMS *Eagle* and *Argus*. By the end of the month, the *Eagle* delivered sixteen more Spitfires to the island.[63]

Kesselring's staff drew up a plan for an increased aerial offensive against Malta, which was designed to destroy the island's offensive and defensive capabilities. This third German air offensive against Malta started on 20 March and continued through to 10 May 1942.[64] Since planning for an invasion of Malta was taking place, Kesselring used this new offensive to prepare the island for such an invasion. Kesselring outlined the three main phases of the offensive:

> Phase 1: neutralization of the anti-aircraft defenses.
> Phase 2: mass attacks against airfields and aircraft.
> Phase 3: attacks against naval forces, dockyards, and installations at La Valetta until completely destroyed.[65]

Even though this was a combined German/Italian operation, the Italian Air Force had such a poor operational readiness rate that it was not expected to take part until phase two began, after the antiaircraft defenses were worn down. Based on Kesselring's plan, the Luftwaffe engaged in "carpet bombing" for the first time against the island. This worked to the Luftwaffe's benefit because it lowered the losses that came from pin point diving attacks and it caused the defenders of Malta to expend far more antiaircraft ammunition against the attacking planes then they had before. By 22 March the Luftwaffe was in command of the air around Malta and even though it had to divert attacks on the 23 March because of the arrival of convoy MW-10, the Axis air forces were able to concentrate their attacks on the bomber and naval bases in and around Grand Harbor.[66] As the raids continued into April, the situation on the island became perilous. General Dobbie, the commander of Malta's forces, reported that the supplies that they had received from individual ships could not be unloaded until air superiority was restored. The status of the island by 12 April showed that ammunition was running very low, and that without replenishment the food would be gone by June. General Dobbie also found it was almost impossible to oppose the Axis aircraft with his shrinking number of fighters.[67]

Attempts were made to provide more fighters to Malta throughout this axis offensive. On 20 April the American aircraft carrier USS *Wasp* ferried forty-seven Spitfires to Malta. All managed to take off and all but one were able to make it safely to the island, however, the German radar had tracked the flight. Within a few hours of the planes landing, German bombers conducted concentrated attacks against the airfields and the aircraft on the ground. Within three days of the aircraft arriving, Malta was reduced to only six serviceable aircraft for defense.[68] By 29 April Kesselring believed that because of the lack of fighter defense, the shortage of antiaircraft ammunition and the destruction of the naval installations, Malta was eliminated as a fighting base. This was relayed to Hitler on 10 May when the offensive ended. This was wishful thinking on Kesselring's part. The British were running out of antiaircraft ammunition but a single ship managed to slip through the Axis air and sea blockade and deliver enough to cause more losses over the next few days then the Germans had suffered during the 11,500 sorties over the previous five weeks. On 9 May the aircraft carriers USS *Wasp* and HMS *Eagle* managed to ferry sixty more Spitfires to Malta, just as the air offensive was coming to a close.[69] These statements by Kesselring would cause problems when the decision to launch Hercules came to a point.

During the air offensive from 20 March to 10 May 1942 the Germans and Italians flew 11,819 sorties: 5,807 by bomber, 5,667 by fighters, and 345 by reconnaissance aircraft, and dropped a total of over 6,577 tons of bombs on Malta.[70] Although the island's installations were severely damaged and unable to conduct any offensive operations, its defenders were not defeated and were given a reprieve when large elements of the II Luftflotte in the form of two groups of Ju-88s and two groups of Me 109s, were transferred to the Russian Front for the summer offensive; while more aircraft were transferred to North Africa for Rommel's upcoming offensive codenamed "Theseus."[71] These transfers reflected the strategic and operational focus of the German High Command.

The Italian Air Force again was left with the main responsibility to ensure that Malta could not mount offensive operations. The Italian Air Staff believed that the remaining German aircraft plus about thirty Italian aircraft would be enough to maintain the neutralization of Malta. With this in mind they still pointed out in a memorandum dated 10 May 1942 that:

> The neutralization of Malta is partial and temporary. …It is necessary to continue and to increase blockade operations by using strong formations against the Eastern and Western approaches…72

As in the spring of 1941 the German leadership managed to give life back to Malta by believing that neutralization meant the destruction of Malta. The British retained and exploited the ability to reinforce and rebuild the defenses and offensive capabilities of Malta. This assumption would significantly impact the planning for the proposed invasion of Malta and the events that would cause its cancellation.

[1]George Forty, *Battle for Malta* (Hersham, England: Ian Allen Publishing. 2003), 52.

[2]Ibid., 23.

[3]Lutton, 25.

[4]Albrecht Kesselring, *The Memoirs of Field Marshal Kesselring* (Novato, CA: Presidio Press, 1989), 123.

[5]Edward Short, "Malta: Strategic Impact During World War II" (Research paper, US Army War College, Carlisle Barracks, 2000), 5.

[6]Lutton, 29.

[7]Forty, 56.

[8]Lutton, 37.

[9]Ibid., 32.

[10]Forty, 27.

[11]Ibid., 35.

[12]Ibid., 52-53.

[13]Lutton, 30-32.

[14]Forty, 29.

[15]Lutton, 36.

[16]Forty, 31-32.

[17]Ibid., 57.

[18]Lutton, 32.

[19]Forty, 57.

[20]Lutton, 33.

[21]Ibid., 36.

[22]Forty, 38.

[23]Lutton, 138.

[24] Forty, 24.

[25] Short, 4.

[26] Horst Boog, Werner Rahn, Reinhard Stumpf, and Bernd Wegner, *Germany and the Second World War,* vol. 6, *The Global War: Widening of the Conflict into a World War and the Shift of the Initiative, 1941-1943* (Oxford, England: Clarendon Press, 2001), 655.

[27] McDonald, http://www.worldwar2database.com/html/africa.htm.

[28] Lutton, 38-39.

[29] Ibid., 44-45.

[30] Short, 5-6.

[31] Schreiber, Stegmann, and Vogel, 661-662.

[32] Short, 7.

[33] Ibid., 7.

[34] Schreiber, Stegmann, and Vogel, 670-671.

[35] Forty, 6.

[36] Ibid., 81.

[37] Lutton, 128.

[38] Ibid., 135-136.

[39] Ibid., 149.

[40] Ibid., 150.

[41] Forty, 81.

[42] Ibid., 114-115.

[43] Lutton, 118-119.

[44] Ibid., 132.

[45] Ibid., 134-135.

[46] Forty, 115.

[47] McDonald, http://www.worldwar2database.com/html/singapore.htm.

[48] Harper Collins, *Atlas of the Second World War* (Ann Arbor, Michigan: Border Press, 2003), 76.

[49] McDonald, http://www.worldwar2database.com/html/india42.htm.

[50] Collins, 88-89.

[51] McDonald, http://www.worldwar2database.com/html/barbarossa.htm.

[52] McDonald, http://www.worldwar2database.com/html/stalingrad.htm.

[53] Lutton, 158.

[54] Ibid., 160.

[55] Ibid., 161.

[56] Ibid., 157-158.

[57] Ibid., 163-164.

[58] Ibid., 168-169.

[59] Forty, 114.

[60] Lutton, 170.

[61] Ibid., 195.

[62] Ibid., 173.

[63] Ibid., 165.

[64] Kesselring, 119.

[65] Lutton, 167.

[66] Ibid., 167-168.

[67] Ibid., 175.

[68] Ibid., 180.

[69] Macksey, 117.

[70] Forty, 68.

[71] Warlimont, 236-237.

[72] Lutton, 180.

CHAPTER 5

OPERATION HERCULES

<u>Planning of Operation</u>

During the planning for Operation Mercury, the German Armed Forces Command, OKW, developed a plan to invade Malta. This plan was dropped in favor of the invasion of Crete based on the decision of Hitler who believed that Crete was of more strategic value. Almost nine months later the idea to invade Malta would come up again and would take into account the lessons learned from the invasion of Crete in May 1941.

While the air offensive against Malta was taking place in the winter of 1942, planning was again underway for an invasion of Malta. The Italians had considered an invasion, and the effectiveness of the Luftwaffe attacks gave the idea new life. Rommel at one point remembered: "The heavy Axis air raids against Malta, in particular, were instrumental in practically neutralizing for a time the threat to our sea routes."[1] The Italians placed the capture of Malta as their number one priority, but knew that they could not conduct the operation on their own. They were also unable to provide a solid date that their forces would be able to conduct an operation.[2] Many German leaders knew that Malta had to be taken to ensure the continued safety of supplies to North Africa. Kesselring, who was a strong supporter of an invasion, believed that it should come quickly after an air bombardment. As the commander on the receiving end of the lack of supplies going to North Africa, because of the attacks against convoys from Malta, Rommel was a strong supporter of an attack to capture the island. He wrote at one point that he offered to carry out an invasion of island, and believed that it would have succeeded.[3] Rommel was anxious to see the island taken because he wanted to start his new offensive as soon as possible after his supplies were replenished. Even before getting the approval of Hitler and Mussolini, the planning for the combined invasion of Malta continued.[4]

Kesselring informed the German Naval staff on 11 March that the Italians were serious about invading Malta and were planning for such an operation. The Italians wanted to take the island as soon as possible and Commando Supremo thought that they would be ready to start the invasion in July 1942. Admiral Raeder, who also supported an invasion of Malta, met with Hitler on 14 March to discuss the need to launch a drive to capture the Suez Canal in 1942. He also pointed out the need to take Malta in order to secure the supply lines for such an operation. Raeder informed Hitler that the favorable situation in the Mediterranean supporting an invasion would not happen again and that failure to capture Malta would seriously complicate the movement of supplies to North Africa.[5] Previously, at a conference in February 1942 between Hitler and Mussolini, the project was approved though the plan had not been settled upon. OKW made the plan official by formally asking Kesselring in March about the feasibility of invading Malta. Kesselring replied on 11 March that the Italians' intended to capture the island, adding that this would be "no problem" and "significantly easier then the seizure of Crete".[6] The fact that Kesselring relayed to both OKW and the Ober Kommando der Kriegsmarine (OKM) on 11 March about the Italians seriousness of invading Malta shows how separated the higher German military leadership was. OKW pressed Kesselring to get an earlier date for the invasion from Cavallero, Chief of Commando Supremo, who agreed to execute the invasion sooner if the Luftwaffe was able to weaken the island to such an extent to ensure success.

On 10 April, the plan to invade Malta was given the codename Hercules by the OKW. In a meeting with Hitler on 12 April Admiral Raeder again urged that Malta must be taken. He pointed out that "Malta will never again be as weak as it is right now," and warned Hitler that "its defenses will be rebuilt immediately if we let up on the present strong attacks." Raeder went on to recommend that Hitler prevail upon the Japanese to launch a naval and air offensive in the western part of the Indian Ocean and the Persian Gulf in order to preoccupy the Royal Navy forces at Alexandria and also compromise Britain's supply lines to the Middle East.[7]

It must be noted that through all the planning for Hercules and right up to the point where it was finally cancelled, Hitler never fully supported the idea of invading Malta. He never gave a reason at the time, but was persuaded to allow the planning and preparations to continue based on the recommendations that it was necessary for the offensive in North Africa to succeed. Because of the limited air assets in the Mediterranean Theater, the Germans had to prioritize the two upcoming operations in the Mediterranean. First was the invasion of Malta that would eliminate the British threat to the Axis supply lines and permit more freedom of movement for Axis forces in the Mediterranean and for Rommel in North Africa. The second was Rommel's planned offensive in North Africa that was supposed to take the port of Tobruk, removing a thorn festering in Rommel's flank since the offensive in 1941. This offensive's ultimate goal was driving all the way into Egypt and capturing Alexandria. Rommel supported taking Malta first. He had seen how the neutralization of the island had benefited his logistics situation. In mid April 1942 Rommel sent a proposal to OKW stating that Malta must be taken before an attack on Tobruk should occur, which must also be taken before an attack on the Nile could be executed.[8] The reasoning behind this proposal was the realization that all the aircraft that were being lost in the air offensive against Malta would subtract from the aircraft to support his own offensive in North Africa, and knowing that if Malta were not taken that it would reemerge to attack his supply lines again. Although this was logical thinking, it would prove fruitless.

At the end of April, Mussolini traveled to Berchtesgaden to meet with Hitler for a planning conference for the upcoming operations in the Mediterranean. During this meeting, a timetable was established for the two operations. Instead of attacking Malta first, Rommel would begin his offensive towards the end of May 1942. He would capture Tobruk and then halt on the Egyptian frontier. This halt was scheduled to take place by 17 June. After that, the Luftwaffe assets would be transferred back to Sicily to conduct raids against Malta prior to the invasion, which was scheduled for on or about 17 July 1942. After Malta was captured, the Luftwaffe assets would be sent back to North Africa to support Rommel's attack to the Nile.[9] Rommel was not at this conference so he was unable to plead his case for the elimination of Malta prior to starting his own offensive. At this meeting, Hitler showed complete public support for Operation Hercules. Cavallero recorded in his diary the outcome of the meeting:

> As to Malta, the Fuehrer is of the opinion that it must be taken from the British. . . . The Fuehrer envisages an operation based on the use of troops landed from gliders, who will pave the way for parachutists. . . . An item of curiosity, I showed the Fuehrer Napoleon's plan of 1798 for the conquest of the island.[10]

On 1 May the German Naval Operations Staff noted in the war diary for that day both the results of the meeting in Berchtesgaden, the view of the Navy towards the sequence of the operations and their continued feelings about Malta:

The Libya operations should be executed first, followed by the Malta operation, since both cannot be conducted simultaneously, especially as regards air support. It is intended to rush some reinforcements to Rommel. They will be numerically small.

The Fuehrer has promised strong German participation in the Malta operation (one parachute division consisting of three reinforced parachute regiments). It is important that the Navy concentrate and make available the largest possible number of naval barges even if this should entail temporary weakening of other areas (Aegean Sea, if necessary even Black Sea).

In spite of these plans, Second Air Fleet will not be able to remain in Italy in full strength but will have to transfer some of its forces primarily to the western area. Evidently, Field Marshal Kesselring thinks that these forces can safely be withdrawn without giving the British defense of Malta a chance to recuperate.

Basically, the Naval Staff is pleased with the greater interest in the Mediterranean war shown by the Fuehrer and the resulting decision for German action in this area; however, with regard to the overall naval situation, it is undesirable to put off the Malta operation.[11]

Hercules: The Plan

By this point, the preparations for the invasion were well underway, and the plan had been solidified and the operation was scheduled to commence on 18 July 1942. The plans of the operation consisted of three main phases and were outlined as such:

    1. Attack by airborne troops of General Student's XI Air Corps(Parachute) to seize the southern heights as a jumping-off base for an assault to capture the airfields south of the town and the harbor of La Valetta, shortly preceded by an intense bombing raid on the airfields themselves and anti-aircraft positions.

    2. Main attack by naval forces and landing parties against the strong-points south of La Valetta and, in conjunction with parachute troops, on the harbor itself, synchronized with bombing raids on coastal batteries. This would create bridgehead to allow the landing of four Italian divisions by ship.

    3. Diversionary attack would be made from the sea against Marsa Scirocco Bay.[12] (see figure 4)

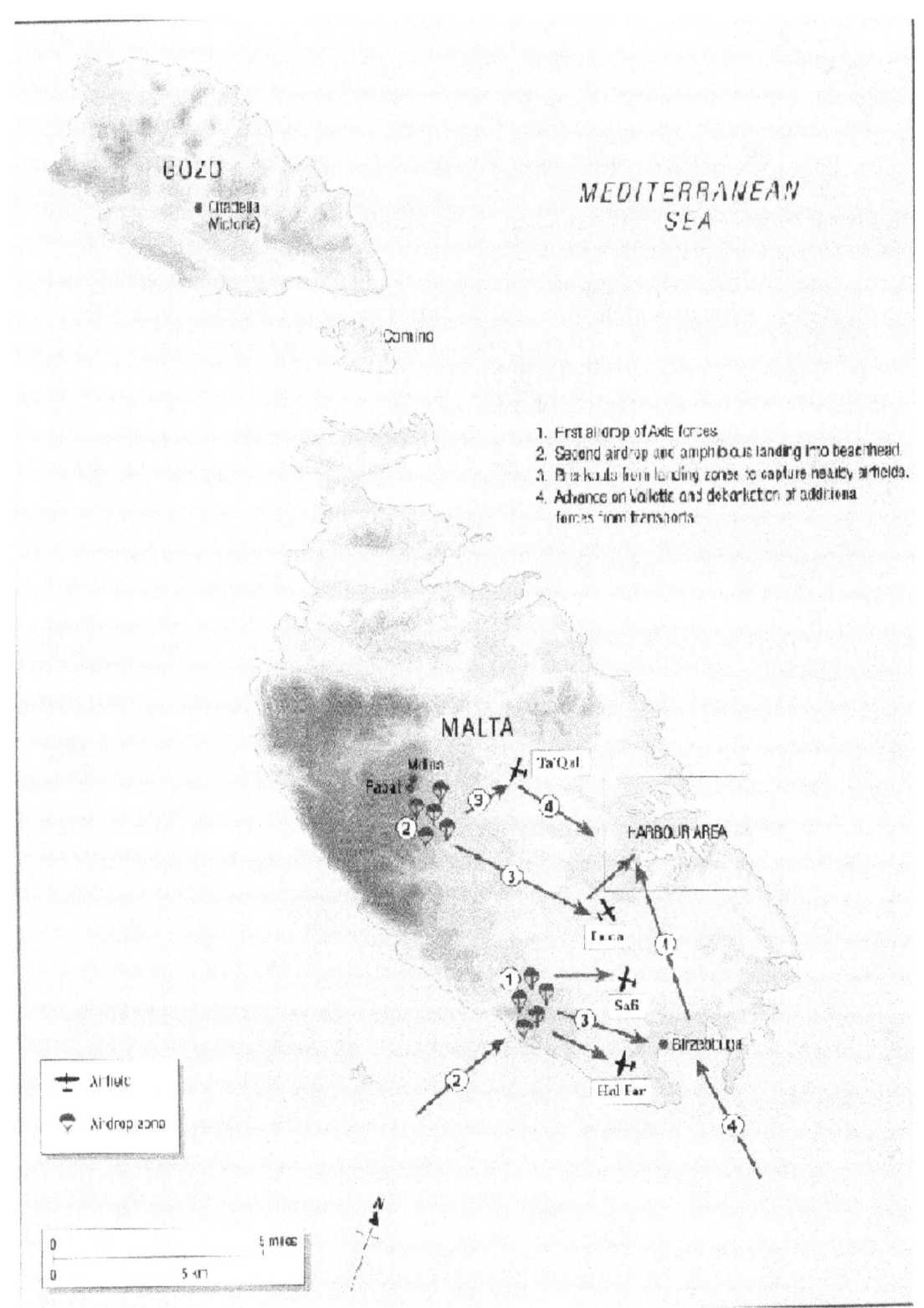

Figure 4. Diagram of Hercules Plan
*Source:*Charles Stephenson, *The Fortifications of Malta 1530-1945*, (Oxford, England: Osprey Publishing, 2004), 55.

Since there was a month scheduled from the ending of Rommel's offensive to the beginning of Hercules, a fourth air offensive was scheduled to prepare the island for invasion. This shaping operation was to take place from 28 June to 17 July once the II *Luftflotte* aircraft moved from North Africa to Sicily. The air offensive was planned in the following terms:

> Once the Luftwaffe had redeployed in Sicily, it would join with Italian units in an all-out bomber and fighter assault on Malta. Day and night raids would take place until command of the air had been achieved.
> During the course of these operations, final low-level reconnaissance would be made of defense installations.
> After air superiority was reestablished (estimated taking a week) the Axis air forces would conduct systematic attacks on all defensive installations. Low level and dive bombing attacks would be made against anti-aircraft batteries, especially those protecting airfields.
> During the second week of the air offensive, depots and barracks would be destroyed. Any targets which could provide cover for tanks were to be given special attention.
> A day before the invasion was to commence, Malta was to be put out of action as a functioning British air base.[13]

Compared to the invasion of Crete, the troops allocated to Hercules were impressive and intended to ensure victory. The order of battle consisted of three separate corps. The first to go in would be General Student's XI Air Corps (Parachute) that consisted of the 7th Flieger Division, with three additional Fallschirmjäger Regiments, the Italian 1st Folgore Parachute Division, and the Italian 80th La Spezia Air Landing Division. Coming in on the first seaborne assault wave was the Italian XXX Army Corps with the 1st Superga, 4th Livorno, and 20th Fruili Infantry Divisions. Along with these divisions the XXX Corps was augmented by the 10th Armored Brigade, the San Marco Naval Infantry Brigade, and the Camicie Nere da Sbarco Infantry Brigade. Following in support in the second seaborne wave was the Italian XVI Army Corps with the 26th

Asseietta and 54th Napoli Infantry Divisions.[14] The Italian divisions slated for the invasion were picked by Kesselring and specially trained to take part in Hercules. The Germans also allocated a mountain division to take part if necessary, but that was not included in either the airborne or seaborne assaults.[15] In total, some 30,000 men were to take part in the airborne assault while a further 70,000 would follow in the seaborne attack. This was a far larger number than was actually used in Operation Mercury the previous year.[16] (see figure 5)

Hercules: Training

Unlike Operation Mercury, which was thrown together in just over six weeks, the troops for Hercules spent almost nine months preparing for the invasion. The 7th Flieger Division was rebuilt after the losses it had suffered in Crete. The German parachute expert, Generalmajor Bernhard Ramcke, was sent to Italy and assigned to train the Italian Folgore Division and the La Spezia Division. According to Ramcke and Student these Italian divisions were much better equipped and trained than the standard Italian infantry divisions and the morale was far higher.[17] At exercises that Field Marshal Kesselring attended he commented that the Italians were the "right material" for the operation and could be considered elite, even by German standards.[18]

Along with the units that would either jump or air land on Malta, training was extensive for the seaborne assault divisions and supporting units. The three infantry divisions planned for the first wave of the seaborne assault were all given special training in their tasks of amphibious landings. The same was done for the San Marco Brigade and the Camicie Nere da Sbarco Infantry Brigade, which were four blackshirt battalions made up of young fascists.[19]

While the training was going on, General Student's staff had looked at the lessons learned from Crete and had made several significant improvements. These improvements dealt with the harness that the paratroopers jumped with, the way the troops carried their weapons and ammunition while jumping, and the uniform they used for jumping.

First, the harness used in Crete resulted in too many unnecessary deaths because its design forced the trooper to have to stand upright to release the parachute and get out of the harness. This was a process that took up to eighty seconds. The fix was a new harness that allowed the paratrooper to release his chute while remaining in the prone position and took only about ten seconds. Second, the paratroopers of the 7th Flieger Division were better armed then the standard infantryman, however, when they jumped onto Crete they did not carry their weapons with them. Instead their weapons were dropped in containers that went out of the plane before the paratrooper and once on the ground the paratroop had to fight his way to the container to get his weapons. This was fixed by increasing the firepower, ensuring that the paratroopers carried automatic weapons and hand grenades when jumping. Finally, the jumpsuit that was used in earlier operations was cumbersome and difficult to wear. The new jumpsuit provided better protection for the face, shoulders, pelvis, knees, and ankles, thus reducing the likelihood of injury while landing.[20]

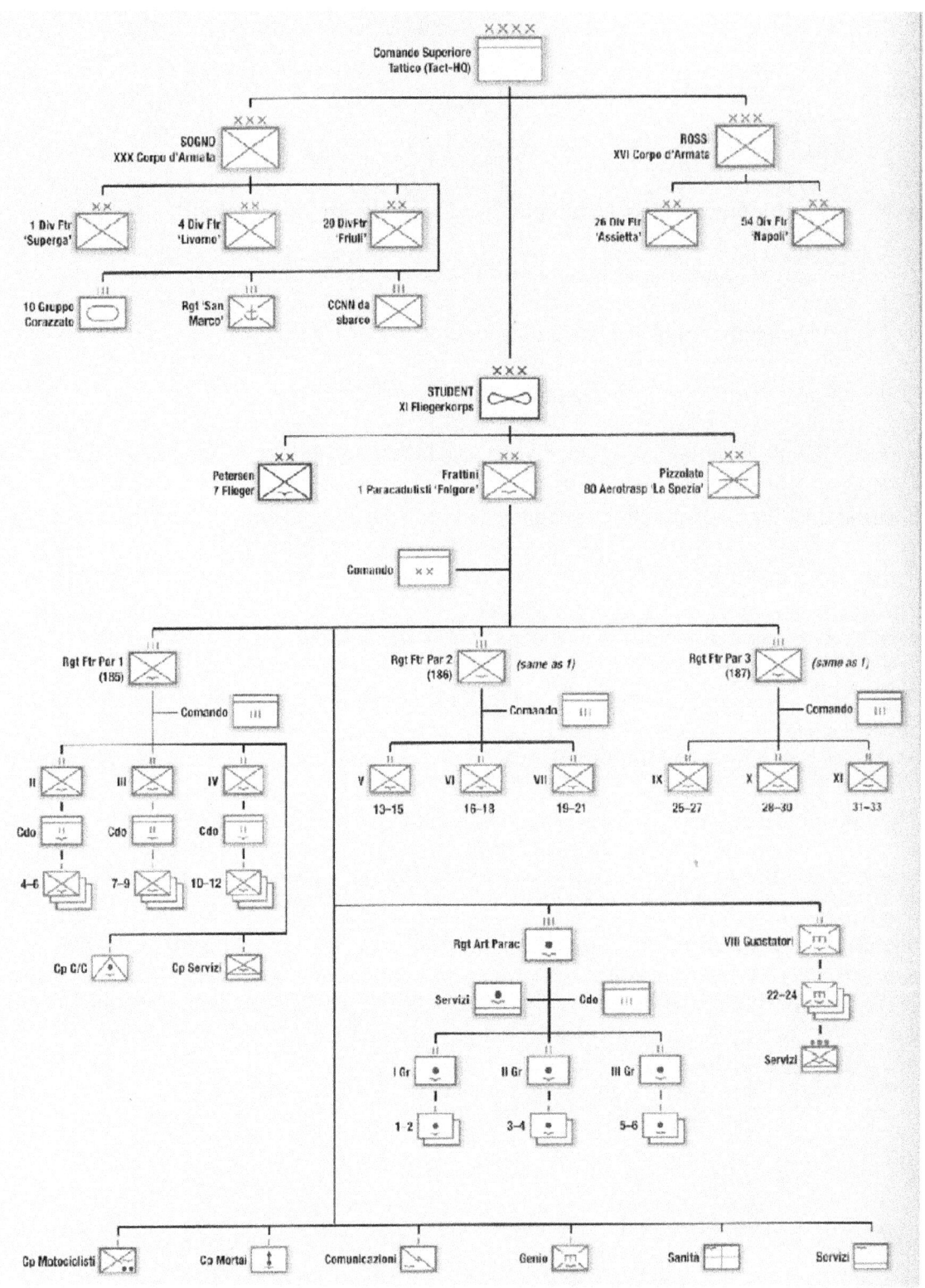

Figure 5. Axis Order of Battle for Operation Hercules
Source: Bruce Quarrie, *German Airborne Divisions: Mediterranean Theatre 1942-1945*. (Oxford, England: Osprey Publishing, 2005), 52.

The training for the invasion continued through June and the view of the German combat leaders was that the invasion would be a success due to the amount of troops allocated and skill of the troops involved. Therefore, the next area to consider is the invasion and logistical support for the forces to get to and survive on the island.

Hercules: Invasion and Logistical Support

The forces to invade Malta had been calculated to ensure that failure was not an option. As compared to 502 Ju-52 aircraft and 100 DFS-230 gliders that had been used in Crete, the Hercules forces had 500 x Ju52 and 12 x Me323 transport aircraft; and 300 x DFS-230 gliders and 200 new Gotha (Go) 242 gliders.[21] The Gotha 242 was a significant increase in the airborne's troop and supply carrying capability. It was capable of carrying twenty-one fully equipped men or four tons of freight. This was as compared to the DFS-230 glider, which could only carry either ten paratroopers or one ton of supplies. The Germans allocated 216 fighters to escort the transports and gliders and 200 other mixed aircraft to support the operation. The Italians allocated 222 fighters and 470 mixed bombers, torpedo-bombers and other assault aircraft.[22]

The task of supporting the seaborne part of the invasion fell mainly on the Italian Navy. To support this part of the invasion they allocated a fleet of merchant vessels, landing craft, and floating barges. To protect these ships, the Italians assigned five battleships, four heavy cruisers, twenty-one destroyers and fourteen submarines along with motor torpedo boats and minesweepers.[23] According to Kesselring, the landing craft were the main sticking point as to when the invasion could be launched. Kesselring impressed upon Raeder that the start date for the invasion was determined by how long it would take the Italians to finish constructing the ferryboats and landing barges. Admiral

Raeder had the OKM and the Naval Construction Division conduct an investigation to determine if the ships would be completed in time. They concluded that they would be completed sooner if more labor was used. Admiral Weichold, the German Naval liaison to the Italian Navy, was told to recommend to the Italian Admiralty an increase in the work force for building these craft.[24]

As part of the preparations for the invasion, the Germans increased their use of jamming. They installed several powerful jamming devices on Sicily to render the British radar on Malta useless. At first this succeeded, but as time went along the British realized what was happening and, after requesting assistance from British Scientific Intelligence, they received the advice to continue to operate as if no jamming was taking place, thereby giving the impression to the Germans that the jamming was not affecting the radar. After a few days of this the Germans turned their jamming devices off.[25]

Rommel Seizes Tobruk

Rommel launched his offensive on 26 May 1942 and initially moved faster then originally planned although the British had numerical superiority. Prior to the start of the offensive, Count Cavallero had emphasized to Rommel that his offensive must be completed by 20 June so that Hercules could begin on time.[26] To support Theseus II Luftflotte transferred 260 aircraft to North Africa. This left 115 aircraft in Sicily to work with the Italians to hinder the British attempts to recover from the April offensive.[27]

While the offensive in North Africa was underway preparations for Hercules continued. The recovery of the Malta defenses also continued. The recovery began as soon as the spring offensive ended on 10 May. On 10 May a single ship brought in more ammunition. With the arrival of this ammunition and over sixty Spitfires at the beginning of May, a visible turning point had occurred in the battle for Malta. On 19 May the II Fliegerkorps reported that daylight bombing was no longer possible because of the increased fighter defenses.[28]

As June 1942 began, Rommel's offensive continued but slowed due to resistance and increasing supply lines. It took four days longer then scheduled but the Africa Corps was still able to capture the port of Tobruk on 21 June 1942.[29] During this offensive, it took less then two days of fighting to capture the port. This was after Tobruk had held out for over eight months during the 1941 campaign. Tobruk fell so quickly that the British were not able to destroy the vast amounts of supplies that were there. Rommel's forces captured over three million rations, 500,000 gallons of fuel, and arms and other equipment that were pressed into service by the Africa Corps. Kesselring visited Rommel the next day at his headquarters in Tobruk. When Kesselring arrived he congratulated Rommel, who had recently been promoted to Field Marshal, and found him briefing his commanders and staff on an advance to Sidi Barani. The same day Rommel also sent a message to the OKW asking for permission to continue his advance, which ran counter to the plan for Hercules:

> The first objective of the Panzer Army in Africa that of defeating the enemy in the field and capturing Tobruk has been achieved. . . . Therefore request that the Duce be prevailed upon to remove the present restriction on movement and that all troops now under my command be placed at my disposal to continue the offensive.[30]

Kesselring did not object to this advance because it "coincided with my views of things without prejudicing the attack on Malta." This request, along with the misgivings of Hitler, would turn Hercules on its head and ultimately cause its cancellation.[31]

Hercules: Cancelled

Hitler had his misgivings about launching Hercules from the beginning. Part of this was his own thinking and part of it came from Goering who thought the island could not be captured because of the many walls and the broken terrain on the island. Neither one had taken the idea seriously and had not listened carefully to the reports of their subordinates about the operational plan.

It is important to note that at times Kesselring did not help the situation because he over emphasized the effects of the bombing on the island, which hurt the cause of the operation. During the offensive against Malta in April 1942 Kesselring announced prematurely to Mussolini and Count Cavallero that "Malta as a naval base no longer demands consideration."[32] Because of Kesselring's statement, he lost some of the support of the Italian leadership and, when he reported that the start of the invasion could be moved up to 31 May, Mussolini and Cavallero changed their minds and claimed that since Malta was not an immediate threat, the original proposed start date was sufficient.

All through this debate, the British continued to reinforce the island. The British War Cabinet decided to send two simultaneous convoys to Malta in June, one from Gibraltar and one from Alexandria. Just prior to the convoys getting underway, the aircraft carrier HMS *Eagle* flew in fifty-nine Spitfires on 3 and 11 June.[33] In the end, only the convoy from Gibraltar made it to Malta with two merchant ships that delivered 25,000 tons of supplies. It lost four merchant ships, one tanker and five escorts. The convoy from Alexandria suffered four warships and two merchant ships sunk, the remainder returning to Alexandria.[34]

Even before these convoys left port, Hitler had expressed his doubts about Hercules. Kesselring thought that part of the doubt was because the plan was not his own or because Hitler did not understand the complete workings of air and sea power, but either way it became evident Hitler was losing confidence in the plan as either a military necessity or for the political need.[35]

In early June, Hitler summoned General Student to his headquarters to get an update on Hercules. The day before Hitler saw Student, he saw General Ludwig Crüwell, one of Rommel's Africa Corps commanders, who gave an unfavorable account about the state of the Italian forces and the quality of the Italian soldier.[36] After General Student gave his briefing to Hitler, he was told that although it would be possible to establish a bridgehead on Malta that it would not be possible to hold it. Hitler warned Student:

> I can assure you, though, that as soon as we begin our attack the Gibraltar squadrons will take to the air and the British fleet will set sail from Alexandria. You can imagine how the Italians will react to that. The minute they get the news on their radios, they'll all make a dash for the harbors of Sicily—both warships and freighters. You'll be sitting all alone on the island with your paratroopers.[37]

After this conference, Student was ordered to not return to Italy and that the planning for Hercules was to continue only on paper. If Rommel succeeded in taking Tobruk the plan would be abandoned because the supply ships could be sent to Tobruk via Crete and Greece.[38] Student did not return to Italy, but he did report back to Kesselring on the recent developments. At that time the official preparations were not abandoned, and Kesselring and Cavallero, who were both intent on executing the operations, continued to prepare.[39]

On 15 June Hitler met with Admiral Raeder to discuss the pro's and con's of Hercules. Hitler informed Raeder that he did not believe that Malta could be taken while the offensive on the Russian Front was ongoing. He especially did not believe it could be taken with Italian forces. Although Raeder agreed with Hitler about the "uncertain quality" of Italian troops, he felt confident that the supplies would get to Malta and that the Luftwaffe could defeat any British attempts to relieve their troops on the island. OKM reported that the operation was risky and difficult, but that it was more risky to "not carry out the operation." As a strategic necessity, the Navy felt that the Axis must seize Malta if Germany wanted to continue to supply its troops in North Africa and to seize the Suez Canal. Finally, the Navy concluded that if Germany waited past the summer to seize Malta the conditions would not allow for success.[40]

So, once Rommel seized Tobruk and requested permission to continue his offensive, it did not take long to get approval. Rommel sent messages to both Hitler and Mussolini requesting to continue the advance. Rommel had to get the approval of Mussolini since the Africa Corps fell under the Italian chain of command. Although the advice from Kesselring, von Rintelen, and the Navy Staff ran opposite to Rommel's request Hitler decided to support Rommel and wrote to Mussolini to persuade him to allow Rommel to resume his offensive. In his note, he wrote "It is only once in a lifetime that the Goddess of Victory smiles."[41] This influenced Mussolini to approve Rommel's request and thus Hercules was abandoned and the capture of the Suez Canal and the defeat of the British in North Africa became the top priority.

Although Hercules was not officially abandoned, the possibility of executing it became more and more problematic. Once Rommel resumed his offensive, Cavallero, who had given Kesselring tacit support for Hercules, was relieved to be rid of the operation and was under instructions from Mussolini to reach for "the political advantage."[42] On 24 June General von Rintelen reported to OKH Operation Division that Mussolini was in "complete agreement with the Fuehrer's opinion and that the historic moment had now come to conquer Egypt and must be exploited."[43] Von Rintelen also pointed out that "owing to Malta's active revival, supply of the Panzer Army in Africa has once more entered a critical stage." He recommended that due to this the II Luftflotte should be reinforced and resume the bombardment of Malta. Because it ran so close to Malta, the Italians were forced to abandon the western supply route to North Africa until the island was neutralized again and they postponed Operation "C.3" (The Italian designation for Hercules) until September 1942.

On 26 June Count Cavallero issued the following instructions from Commando Supremo for the continued battle in Egypt:

>1. The situation of the British 8th Army demands that successes gained so far be exploited as far as possible.
>2. In spite of this it must be taken into consideration that the supply problem offers difficulties. The air base of Malta has resumed offensive operations. The Tripoli route must be temporarily abandoned and the route to harbors in Cyrenaica is also endangered. It is planned to neutralize Malta again, employing formations to be transferred from Germany. This, however, requires more time, during which a critical period cannot be avoided.[44]

On 7 July Cavallero ordered the combined Malta invasion staff to prepare for the transfer of men to Tunisia. By the middle of July several key units earmarked for Hercules such as General Ramcke's Parachute Brigade and the Italian Folgore Division were sent to support Rommel's move into Egypt. Then on 21 July OKM sent out a message stating that Hercules would not occur until Theseus was completed. The next day another message was issued saying that Hercules was "suspended until further notice" and "if a deadline for the execution of the operation was re-established, the necessary measures would be taken." Captain Wolf Junge, a naval staff officer at Hitler's Headquarters, noted, "so Hercules simply fell under the table."[45]

What Happened to Malta?

Even though Hercules was cancelled, Malta was not out of danger. The aerial bombardment began again and Malta was still faced with the possibility of being forced to surrender from starvation. Supplies were running drastically short because of the German and Italian air interdiction of the last few convoys and more supplies were necessary if Malta was to be able to maintain its offensive capabilities. The British War Cabinet decided to send another convoy to resupply Malta in August. This was the largest convoy of the war to go to Malta. Codenamed Operation Pedestal it involved fourteen fast cargo ships and the oil tanker *Ohio*. These ships carried 140,000 tons of supplies for Malta. The Ohio was the sister ship of the tanker *Kentucky*, which had been sunk in the June convoy.[46] Only four ships reached Malta. Two of them, including the *Ohio*, arrived in sinking condition; however, they did bring in 12,000 tons of fuel oil, 3,600 tons of diesel oil and 32,000 tons of general supplies. This was the last convoy to arrive at Malta until the Torch Landings occurred in November 1942, but it was sufficient to sustain the island, which was fifteen days past the estimated point of starvation when the ships arrived.[47]

Kesselring began a last offensive against Malta in October 1942. The Axis air forces flew over 1400 sorties against the island but the defending British spitfires and anti-aircraft gunners took such a heavy toll that the offensive was cancelled after only two weeks. After this, Kesselring was forced by circumstances to provide increased air escorts to the supply convoys going to North Africa.[48]

With General Montgomery's offensive at El Alamein in late October, the Torch landings in the first week of November 1942, and the arrival of a supply convoy in November and another in December 1942, the siege of Malta was effectively over.[49] Hitler had several opportunities to defeat Malta and, for reasons that he thought were more important, passed them by.

---

[1]Matthew Cooper, *The German Army 1933-1945: Its Political and Military Failure* (Chelsea, Michigan: Scarborough House. 1990), 368.

[2]Warlimont, 236.

[3]B. H. Liddell-Hart, *The Rommel Papers* (New York: Da Capa Press, 1953), 288.

[4]Cooper, 368-369.

[5]Lutton, 166.

[6]Macksey, 115.

[7]Lutton, 173-174.

[8]Macksey, 116.

[9]Liddell-Hart, *The Rommel Papers*, 203.

[10]Lutton, 177.

[11]Ibid., 178.

[12]Kesselring, 128.

[13]Lutton, 189.

[14]Quarrie, 52-53.

[15]Forty, 60.

[16]Ibid., 64.

[17]Lutton, 183-184.

[18]Kesselring, 128.

[19] Lutton, 184.

[20] Ibid., 184-185.

[21] Forty, 60-64.

[22] Lutton, 185.

[23] Forty, 64.

[24] Lutton, 174.

[25] Forty, 66.

[26] Lutton, 182-183.

[27] Macksey, 117.

[28] Lutton, 182.

[29] Ibid., 198-199.

[30] Ibid., 199.

[31] Kesselring, 127-128.

[32] Macksey, 115-116.

[33] Lutton, 196.

[34] Forty, 114.

[35] Macksey, 115.

[36] Liddell Hart, *The German Generals Talk*, 161.

[37] Lutton, 194.

[38] Liddell-Hart, *The Rommel Papers*, 203.

[39] Lutton, 194.

[40] Ibid., 194-195.

[41] Cooper, 369.

[42] Macksey, 122.

⁴³Lutton, 202-203.

⁴⁴Ibid., 204.

⁴⁵Ibid., 206.

⁴⁶Ibid., 207.

⁴⁷Ibid., 212.

⁴⁸Ibid., 216.

⁴⁹Forty, 114.

CHAPTER 6

CONCLUSION

Why Not Malta?

Why did Hitler decide not to attack Malta? Why, after all his senior leaders recommended seizing Malta and after he was critical of Mussolini for not seizing the island in 1940 did Hitler cancel an operation that was well planned and resourced? Experts can raise different arguments about this topic. Some could say that his focus was only in the east and defeating the Soviet Union and that everything else came second. This is true, but when Hercules was first postponed, Hitler's forces in the Soviet Union were driving the Soviets back toward the Volga and had not yet begun their fight in Stalingrad.

The primary reason that Hitler decided against invading Malta was not a singular focus on the Soviet Union but rather a lack of trust. Hitler did not trust his ally Mussolini nor the Italian armed forces. There are several examples in this text that demonstrate how Mussolini made decisions that resulted in the use of German forces to fix the situation and at times prevent the collapse of Italian forces. It was from these observations that Hitler decided to recommend the continuation of the attack in North Africa and the cancellation of the invasion of Malta

From the time that Italy entered the war in June 1940, it had only defeats to show for the lives and resources expended. At the beginning, Italy was driven back into its own territory by the French who were on the verge of collapse against the Germans. When Italy invaded Greece it was pushed back into Albania and was kept on the defensive until Germany invaded the Balkans in April 1941 and conquered Greece. In North Africa, after a short offensive in September 1940 into Egypt, the British counterattacked and defeated the Italian Army, capturing over 100,000 Italians and thus forcing Hitler to send Rommel's Africa Corps to "support" the Italians and prevent the collapse of Mussolini's government.

So, why did Hitler not see that under German leadership and with German troops Malta could be captured? The Luftwaffe had proven during two major air offensives against the island that it could neutralize Malta's defensive and offensive capabilities. At the end of both offensives, the island was in a situation identical to what Kesselring said was needed for an invasion, but both times Hitler decided that the decisive point was elsewhere. The success of these air offensives also worked against an invasion. Hitler thought that if the island could be neutralized by airpower then why should extra resources be used to capture it? This would be a valid argument if an air offensive was sustained, which never happened. Both times that the Luftwaffe pushed Malta to the brink of defeat the offensives were cancelled and the Luftwaffe forces were transferred to the east.

The victory on Crete was another example that worked against capturing Malta. The invasion of Crete was pyrrhic at best. Because the Germans controlled the island and the British had to evacuate, it was considered a victory but at a high price. General Student's forces on Crete suffered over 6,000 casualties, more than twenty-five percent of the total force involved in the operation. Because of these losses, Hitler said that the day of the paratrooper was over and that no large operations would be conducted in the future. However, by the time that General Student spoke with Hitler in June 1942 the 7th *Flieger* Division was rebuilt and had incorporated lessons learned from the Crete operation into its training for Malta. Again it was made very clear to General Student why Hitler would not approve of the operation. Hitler did not trust the Italian Navy.

Hitler told General Student that the Italians would run as soon as the British Navy arrived and that Student's paratroopers would be abandoned on the island. The Italian Navy's fighting quality had always been in question. Both the German naval leaders had expressed doubts regarding the Italian sailors' fighting quality, and the action against the British convoy MW10 in March 1942 showed it clearly. The Italians were able to inflict some damage on the British ships, but were not able to pursue the enemy and decisively defeat the British.

Within a month after the cancellation of Hercules the British had reasserted their ability to attack the Axis convoys and the ground forces in North Africa with devastating effects. In July 1942 only twenty percent of the supplies sent to North Africa actually reached their destination due to British air attacks. Aircraft from Malta were able to operate almost unopposed because the Luftwaffe was exhausted from the fight for Tobruk. This resulted in constant attacks against German ground and sea lines of communications.[1]

The last questions to consider are whether an invasion of Malta would have succeeded and what did the British already know about the coming invasion. These questions are now moot but looking at them adds to the debate. Considering the first question, given the size of the attacking forces, especially the airborne assault, compared to the number and condition of the defenders it is quite possible that the attack would have succeeded. The German airborne forces were well trained and organized and had gained much experience from the invasion of Crete. The Italian forces were hand picked by Kesselring and had gone through the same extensive training as their German counterparts. According to the German leaders these units were fully capable of executing the mission.

Considering the second question, Ultra was the one issue that could not be considered by the German leaders. The Germans thought all their communications were secured through the Enigma machine; however, the British were able to read the German message traffic with complete reliability. This was particularly true of the German Naval and Luftwaffe communications that could not use landline. The German leadership was unaware that the British knew of every convoy that sailed to North Africa and they knew how much of the supplies actually made it to the Axis forces.[2] When it came to planning for Hercules, the British had learned about the invasion through Ultra, although it would be interesting to determine which British officials were informed, and how much they knew. From the beginning, the British knew about the status of the Axis preparations and had started anti-invasion preparations. After the fall of Crete, the British took their own lessons learned and incorporated them into the defense of Malta. Fortunately for the British, they never had to test their defenses because Hitler decided to only permit the "paper" preparations for Malta's invasion.[3]

The last basic point to take from this research is how it relates to today's Contemporary Operating Environment. First, it is necessary to have a clear strategy when conducting a campaign and to ensure that at the end of the campaign you have reached your results. The Axis never reached their goal of neutralizing Malta and every time that the bombing stopped the British rebuilt and continued offensive operations. The second point is to know that the enemy will always have a say in your decisions. Senior leaders must keep an open mind and maintain a realistic approach to conducting operations because unless you completely destroy an enemy, they will attempt to reassert themselves into your operations. The Axis never ensured that the British offensive capabilities on Malta were completely destroyed and, by failing to capture the island, never did the one thing that would ensure security of their own forces in North Africa.

---

[1]Kenneth Macksey, *Kesselring, German Master Strategist of the Second World War* (London, England: Greenhill Books, 1996), 123.

[2]Ibid., 122.

[3]Forty, 66.

BIBLIOGRAPHY

Books

Antill, Peter. *Crete 1941: Germany's Lightning Airborne Assault*. Oxford, England: Osprey Publishing, 2005.

Austin, Douglas. *Malta and British Strategic Policy 1925-1943*. London: Frank Cass, 2004.

Boog, Horst; Werner Rahn, Reinhard Stumpf, and Bernd Wegner. *Germany and the Second World War*. Vol 6, *The Global War: Widening of the Conflict into a World War and the Shift of the Initiative, 1941-1943*. Oxford, England: Clarendon Press, 2001.

Burdick, Charles, ed. *The Halder War Diary, 1939-1942*. Novato, CA: Presidio Press, 1988.

Collins, Harold. *Atlas of the Second World War*. Ann Arbor, MI: Borders Press, 2003.

Cooper, Matthew. *The German Army 1933-1945: Its Political and Military Failure*. Chelsea, MI: Scarborough House, 1990.

Forty, George. *Battle for Malta*. Hersham, England: Ian Allen Publishing, 2003.

Keegan, John. *The Price of Admiralty: The Evolution of Naval Warfare*. London: Penguin Press, 1990.

Kesselring, Albrecht. *The Memoirs of Field Marshal Kesselring*. Novato, CA: Presidio Press, 1989.

Liddell-Hart, B. H. *The German Generals Talk*. New York: Perennial, 2002.

Liddell-Hart, B. H, ed. *The Rommel Papers*. New York: Da Capa Press, 1953.

Lucas, James. *Storming Eagles: German Airborne Forces in World War II*. Edison, NJ: Castle Books, 2004.

Lucas, Laddie. *Malta-the Thorn in Rommel's Side: Six Months that Turned the War*. London: Stanley Paul, 1992.

Lutton, Wayne. *Malta and the Mediterranean: A Study in The Allied and Axis Strategy, Planning, and Intelligence during The Second World War*. Ann Arbor, MI: University Microfilms International, 1983.

Macksey, Kenneth. *Kesselring, German Master Strategist of the Second World War*. London: Greenhill Books, 1996.

Quarrie, Bruce. *German Airborne Divisions: Mediterranean Theatre, 1942-1945.* Oxford, England: Osprey Publishing, 2005.

Schreiber, Gerhard; Bernd Stegemann, and Detlef Vogel. *Germany and the Second World War.* Vol. 3, *The Mediterranean, South-East Europe, and North Africa, 1939-1941.* Oxford, England: Clarendon Press, 1995.

Stephenson, Charles. *The Fortifications of Malta 1530-1945*, Oxford, England: Osprey Publishing, 2004

Warlimont, Walter. *Inside Hitler's Headquarters, 1939-1945.* Novato, CA: Presidio Press, 1964.

Research Papers

Biank, Maria A. "The Battle of Crete: Hitler's Airborne Gamble." MMAS thesis, Command and General Staff College, Fort Leavenworth, KS, 2003.

Short, Edward C. "Malta: Strategic Impact During World War II." Research Paper, U.S. Army War College, Carlisle Barracks. 2000.

Government Documents

Department of the Army. Pamphlet No 20-260, *Historical Study: The German Campaigns in the Balkans (Spring 1941).* Washington, DC: Center for Military History, November 1953. Archives, Combined Arms Research Library, Fort Leavenworth, Kansas.

_____. Pamphlet No 20-232. *Historical Study: Airborne Operations; A German Appraisal.* Washington D.C.: Center for Military History, October 1951. Archives Combined Arms Research Library, Fort Leavenworth, Kansas.

Internet Sources

McDonald, Jason. *The World War II Multimedia Database.* Database on-line. Available from http://www.worldwar2database.com/html. Internet. Accessed on December 2005.

Wikipedia: The Free Encyclopedia. Database on-line. Available from http://en.wikipedia.org/wiki. Internet. Accessed on February 2006.

Adolf Hitler.ws: An Apolitical Historical Website. Database on-line. Available from http://www.adolfhitler.ws/lib/proc/pactofsteel.html. Internet. Accessed on February 2006.

INITIAL DISTRIBUTION LIST

Combined Arms Research Library
U.S. Army Command and General Staff College
250 Gibbon Ave.
Fort Leavenworth, KS 66027-2314

Defense Technical Information Center/OCA
825 John J. Kingman Rd., Suite 944
Fort Belvoir, VA 22060-6218

Dr. Jonathan M. House
DMH
USACGSC
1 Reynolds Ave.
Fort Leavenworth, KS 66027-1352

Mr. Bob A. King
DJMO
USACGSC
1 Reynolds Ave.
Fort Leavenworth, KS 66027-1352

Mr. Herbert F. Merrick
DJMO
USACGSC
1 Reynolds Ave.
Fort Leavenworth, KS 66027-1352

COL Rainer Waelde
German LNO CAC
415 Sherman Ave.
Fort Leavenworth, KS 66027-1352

CERTIFICATION FOR MMAS DISTRIBUTION STATEMENT

1. Certification Date: 16 June 2006

2. Thesis Author: MAJ Stephen L. W. Kavanaugh

3. Thesis Title: Comparison of the Invasion of Crete and the Proposed Invasion of Malta

4. Thesis Committee Members: _____
   Signatures: _____
   _____

5. Distribution Statement: See distribution statements A-X on reverse, then circle appropriate distribution statement letter code below:

(A) B C D E F X   SEE EXPLANATION OF CODES ON REVERSE

If your thesis does not fit into any of the above categories or is classified, you must coordinate with the classified section at CARL.

6. Justification: Justification is required for any distribution other than described in Distribution Statement A. All or part of a thesis may justify distribution limitation. See limitation justification statements 1-10 on reverse, then list, below, the statement(s) that applies (apply) to your thesis and corresponding chapters/sections and pages. Follow sample format shown below:

EXAMPLE

Limitation Justification Statement	/	Chapter/Section	/	Page(s)
Direct Military Support (10)	/	Chapter 3	/	12
Critical Technology (3)	/	Section 4	/	31
Administrative Operational Use (7)	/	Chapter 2	/	13-32

Fill in limitation justification for your thesis below:

Limitation Justification Statement	/	Chapter/Section	/	Page(s)
_____	/	_____	/	_____
_____	/	_____	/	_____
_____	/	_____	/	_____
_____	/	_____	/	_____
_____	/	_____	/	_____

7. MMAS Thesis Author's Signature: _____

STATEMENT A: Approved for public release; distribution is unlimited. (Documents with this statement may be made available or sold to the general public and foreign nationals).

STATEMENT B: Distribution authorized to U.S. Government agencies only (insert reason and date ON REVERSE OF THIS FORM). Currently used reasons for imposing this statement include the following:

    1. Foreign Government Information. Protection of foreign information.

    2. Proprietary Information. Protection of proprietary information not owned by the U.S. Government.

    3. Critical Technology. Protection and control of critical technology including technical data with potential military application.

    4. Test and Evaluation. Protection of test and evaluation of commercial production or military hardware.

    5. Contractor Performance Evaluation. Protection of information involving contractor performance evaluation.

    6. Premature Dissemination. Protection of information involving systems or hardware from premature dissemination.

    7. Administrative/Operational Use. Protection of information restricted to official use or for administrative or operational purposes.

    8. Software Documentation. Protection of software documentation - release only in accordance with the provisions of DoD Instruction 7930.2.

    9. Specific Authority. Protection of information required by a specific authority.

    10. Direct Military Support. To protect export-controlled technical data of such military significance that release for purposes other than direct support of DoD-approved activities may jeopardize a U.S. military advantage.

STATEMENT C: Distribution authorized to U.S. Government agencies and their contractors: (REASON AND DATE). Currently most used reasons are 1, 3, 7, 8, and 9 above.

STATEMENT D: Distribution authorized to DoD and U.S. DoD contractors only; (REASON AND DATE). Currently most reasons are 1, 3, 7, 8, and 9 above.

STATEMENT E: Distribution authorized to DoD only; (REASON AND DATE). Currently most used reasons are 1, 2, 3, 4, 5, 6, 7, 8, 9, and 10.

STATEMENT F: Further dissemination only as directed by (controlling DoD office and date), or higher DoD authority. Used when the DoD originator determines that information is subject to special dissemination limitation specified by paragraph 4-505, DoD 5200.1-R.

STATEMENT X: Distribution authorized to U.S. Government agencies and private individuals of enterprises eligible to obtain export-controlled technical data in accordance with DoD Directive 5230.25; (date). Controlling DoD office is (insert).